# COMPREHENSIVE PRACTICE FOR THE TOEIC® L&R TEST



**Jonathan Lynch　Kotaro Shitori**

**photographs by**
© iStockphoto.com

**音声ファイルのダウンロード／ストリーミング**

CDマーク表示がある箇所は、音声を弊社HPより無料でダウンロード／ストリーミングすることができます。下記URLの書籍詳細ページに音声ダウンロードアイコンがございますのでそちらから自習用音声としてご活用ください。

**https://seibido.co.jp/ad719**

**COMPREHENSIVE PRACTICE FOR THE TOEIC® L&R TEST**
**TOEIC® L&R TEST 600点への徹底演習**

# はじめに

今から10年以上前のことになりますが、当時3年生だったある学生さんが授業の後でTOEICの勉強方法について質問しに来ました。詳しくお話を伺うと、研究室の先生から就職先を紹介され、数カ月以内にある点数以上のTOEICスコアの提出を条件として求められたということでした。その学生さんは早速、お薦めした問題集を購入して一生懸命勉強に励んだようですが、時間が限られていたせいもあり、結局その点数には届かず、その会社に入ることは叶いませんでした。「先生、ダメでした」と報告しに来てくれたときの悲しさと恥ずかしさが入り混じったその表情を、今でも鮮明に覚えています。

TOEICは、世界の160カ国で実施されている、リスニング・セクションとリーディング・セクションからなる約2時間の試験で、日本の企業も数多く利用しています。効率よく英文内容を把握する能力が求められるため、皆さんが受験した（かもしれない）共通テストの英語の延長線上にあると考えてもよいでしょう。TOEICの試験対策をすることによって、大量の情報を瞬時に処理することが求められる現代社会を生き抜くために必要な能力を養うことができます。

TOEICの問題には一定のパターンが存在していますし、解答する際のテクニックなどもある程度知られていますので、練習問題を数多くこなせばこなすほど、それに比例してスコアも着実に上がっていきます。たしかに個人差はあるかもしれませんが、途中で諦めずに地道に努力を続けてさえいけば、誰でも目標のスコアに近づくことができるでしょう。

本テキストは、実際のTOEIC L&R TESTを可能な限り忠実に再現することを目指して作成されました。まずは授業を通じてTOEICそのものに関心を持ち、テストの受験を念頭に高得点を目指して、授業の単位が無事取得できたあとも、各自で学習を継続してもらえたら、著者としてこれ以上の喜びはありません。

この教科書を手にした学生の皆さんには、TOEICのスコアが入りたい会社に自分をアピールするためのひとつの武器となりますように、会社が求めるスコアに達していないという理由だけで、入りたかった会社や就きたかった仕事を諦めるようなことがありませんように、心から強く願っています。

最後になりましたが、本テキストの出版に際し、成美堂編集部の田村栄一氏と松本風見さんには大変御世話になりました。この場を借りて心より御礼申し上げます。有難うございました。

Jonathan Lynch
委文　光太郎

# 本書の使い方

## Vocabulary Exercise

ユニットのリスニング・セクションとリーディング・セクションで使用されている、TOEIC でもよく登場する重要な単語や熟語が選び出されています。それぞれの正しい意味を、a ~ j から選んでください。もし間違えた語句があったときは、その場でしっかり意味を覚えた上で、演習問題に進んでいきましょう。

## LISTENING SECTION

### Dictation Exercise

リスニング問題のウォームアップとして用意されています。音声を聞いて空欄を埋めてください。

### Part 1~4

各パートに Study Point（解法のヒント）と演習問題をそれぞれ用意しています。まずは、問題を解き始める前に Study Point を参照すると、問題に取り組みやすくなるかもしれません。

## READING SECTION

### Part 5~7

ここでも各パートに Study Point（解法のヒント）と演習問題がそれぞれ用意されています。なお、Part 5 の Study Point では、毎回1つの文法事項をピックアップして、例文を提示しながら要点を丁寧に説明しています。

### Review Exercise

Part 7の演習問題で使用された英文を要約したものが提示されています。このパートはリーディング・セクションの中でも特に難易度が高いので、間違えた問題があった場合は、そのままにしておかないことが大切です。この穴埋め問題のエクササイズを通して、Part 7 の本文の内容がしっかり理解できるようによく復習してください。

# CONTENTS

# リンガポルタのご案内

**リンガポルタ連動テキストをご購入の学生さんは、**
**「リンガポルタ」を無料でご利用いただけます！**

本テキストで学習していただく内容に準拠した問題を、オンライン学習システム「リンガポルタ」で学習していただくことができます。PCだけでなく、スマートフォンやタブレットでも学習できます。単語や文法、リスニング力などをよりしっかり身に付けていただくため、ぜひ積極的に活用してください。

リンガポルタの利用にはアカウントとアクセスコードの登録が必要です。登録方法については下記ページにアクセスしてください。

**https://www.seibido.co.jp/linguaporta/register.html**

本テキスト「COMPREHENSIVE PRACTICE FOR THE TOEIC® L&R TEST」のアクセスコードは下記です。

**7314-2049-1231-0365-0003-0086-Z7HJ-YMKK**

・リンガポルタの学習機能（画像はサンプルです。また、すべてのテキストに以下の4つの機能が用意されているわけではありません）

**● 多肢選択**

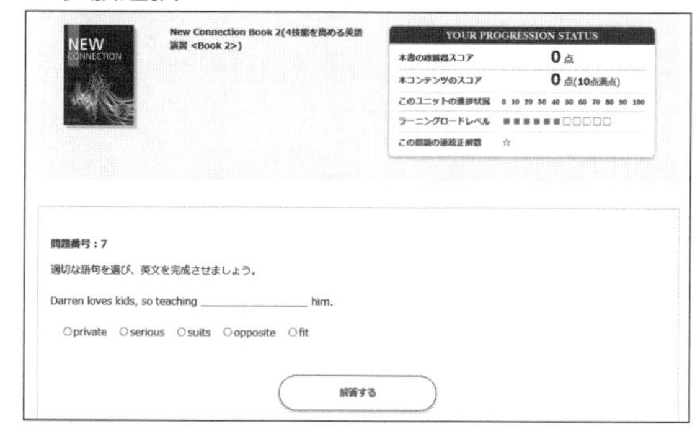


**● 空所補充（音声を使っての聞き取り問題も可能）**

New Connection Book 2(4技能を高める英語演習 <Book 2>)

YOUR PROGRESSION STATUS

問題番号：3

音声を聞いて、空所に当てはまる表現を書き入れましょう。

I'll move my ______ ______ my apartment later.

解答する

**● 単語並びかえ（マウスや手で単語を移動）**

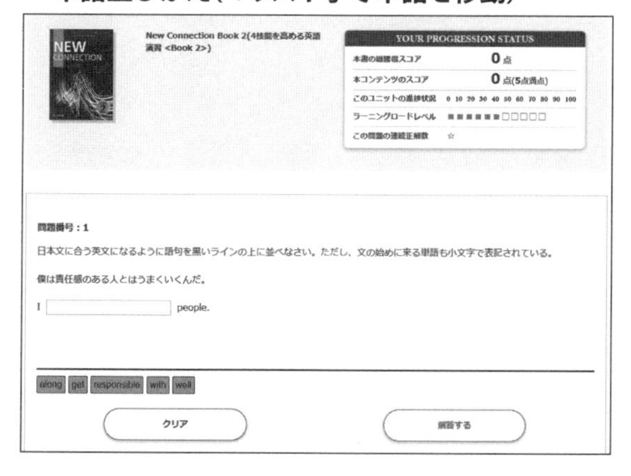


**● マッチング（マウスや手で単語を移動）**

問題番号：4

Match the following English with its Japanese definition.

banking
billboard
award
behave
bargain

お買い得品
賞を与える
ビルボード
ふるまう
銀行の業務

解答する

UNIT 01

# Travel

## Vocabulary Exercise

***Match each English word with its meaning in Japanese.***

**1.** inquiry (　　)　**2.** book (　　)　**3.** luggage (　　)　**4.** itinerary (　　)
**5.** approximately (　　)　**6.** business trip (　　)　**7.** board (　　)
**8.** shortage (　　)　**9.** refreshments (　　)　**10.** refund (　　)

a. 手荷物　b. 予約する　c. 払い戻し　d. 旅行日程（表）　e. およそ
f. 乗り込む　g. 出張　h. 問い合わせ　i. 軽い飲食物　j. 不足

# LISTENING SECTION

## Dictation Exercise

***Listen to the following sentences. Fill in the blank spaces.***

1. Safety ____________________ for our hotel are written on a sign next to the door of your room.
2. I need some ___________ after that long flight. It was 14 hours!
3. When our train _____________ the station, let's get off as quickly as possible.
4. The airplane was scheduled to __________ at 3:00 P.M. but, due to a delay, it will leave 30 minutes later than expected.
5. It is recommended that you keep your seat belt _______________ for the full duration of the flight.

**Study Point**　**Part 1　写真描写問題**

このパートの写真には、**人物**が写っている場合と、**風景や物**だけが写っている場合の 2 種類があります。人物が写っているときは、音声が流れる前に、次のことを行ってください。

**1.** 目立つ人（1 人または複数）に注目します。
**2.「誰（その目立つ人）が」「どこで」「何を」**しているのか確認します。

例）A man is waiting for a train on the platform.
**「誰が」**　**「何を」**　**「どこで」**

## Part 1 Photographs

1-03, 04

***Look at the picture and listen to four statements. Choose one statement that best describes the situation in the picture.***

1.

Ⓐ Ⓑ Ⓒ Ⓓ

2.

Ⓐ Ⓑ Ⓒ Ⓓ

### Study Point Part 2 応答問題

このパートでは疑問文がよく登場します。まずは疑問文の冒頭が What / Who / When / Why / Where / Which / How のどれなのかを聞き分けしましょう。

例 1) **What's** the name of our tour guide? — I haven't met him yet.
例 2) **Who's** picking us up at the station? — Susan is, I think.
例 3) **When** should we leave for the airport? — As soon as we finish packing.
例 4) **Why** did you cancel your trip to Peru? — Because I had an emergency at work.
例 5) **Where's** the best place to visit in this area? — I'm sorry, I'm new here.
例 6) **Which** hotel would you like to stay at? — The one near Central Station.
例 7) **How** are you traveling to the island? — There are regular ferry services.

＊右側の文は正解例です。

## Part 2 Question-Response

1-05～09

*Listen to a question or statement and three responses. Choose the best response to the question or statement.*

3. Mark your answer on your answer sheet. Ⓐ Ⓑ Ⓒ
4. Mark your answer on your answer sheet. Ⓐ Ⓑ Ⓒ
5. Mark your answer on your answer sheet. Ⓐ Ⓑ Ⓒ
6. Mark your answer on your answer sheet. Ⓐ Ⓑ Ⓒ
7. Mark your answer on your answer sheet. Ⓐ Ⓑ Ⓒ

### Study Point Part 3 会話問題

このパートでは 2 人または 3 人の会話が流れます。音声が流れる前に設問をさっと読んで、以下のように**聞き取るポイント**を押さえたり、**話の内容を予測**しましょう。

例 1) **Where do the speakers most likely work?**
→ 会話をしている人たちが働いている**場所**に注目します。

例 2) **What is the woman surprised about?**
→ 会話の中で**女性が何かに驚いている**ことが予測できます。

例 3) **What does the man offer to do?**
→ 会話の中で**男性が相手に何かを申し出ている**ことが予測できます。

## Part 3 Conversation

1-10,11

*Listen to a conversation between two people. Read the questions on your answer sheet. Choose the best answer for each question.*

8. Where does the conversation most likely take place?
(A) At a hotel
(B) In a taxi
(C) On an airplane
(D) On a train
Ⓐ Ⓑ Ⓒ Ⓓ

9. What does the woman offer to do?
(A) Make a hotel reservation
(B) Send an e-mail
(C) Watch a presentation
(D) Call a taxi
Ⓐ Ⓑ Ⓒ Ⓓ

10. What will the man most likely do next?
(A) Open a file on his computer
(B) Check the clients' information
(C) Make a presentation
(D) Change into a business suit
Ⓐ Ⓑ Ⓒ Ⓓ

## Study Point　Part 4 説明文問題

このパートでは、トークが始まる前に次のような指示文が読み上げられます。

Questions 11 through 13 refer to the following announcement.
（お知らせ）

下線部分はトークの内容によって異なるので、内容を予測する上でヒントになることがあります。よく使用される文言は以下の通りです。

... the following ***broadcast***（放送）/ ***advertisement***（広告）/ ***excerpt from a meeting***（会議の抜粋）/ ***telephone message***（留守番電話のメッセージ）/ ***introduction***（紹介）/ ***instructions***（説明）/ ***podcast***（ポッドキャスト）/ ***news report***（ニュース報道）

## Part 4 Talk

***Listen to a talk given by a single speaker. Read the questions on your answer sheet. Choose the best answer for each question.***

**11.** Who most likely is the speaker?
(A) An aircraft mechanic
(B) A travel agent
(C) A flight attendant
(D) An airline pilot
Ⓐ Ⓑ Ⓒ Ⓓ

**12.** What is the reason for the announcement?
(A) Bad weather
(B) Crew shortage
(C) Airplanes ahead
(D) Mechanical problems
Ⓐ Ⓑ Ⓒ Ⓓ

**13.** What does the speaker ask the listeners to do?
(A) Ask for a refund
(B) Call their family members
(C) Put away their laptops
(D) Remain seated
Ⓐ Ⓑ Ⓒ Ⓓ

# READING SECTION

## Study Point Part 5 短文穴埋め問題

### 未来表現

**現在形** 確定している未来の予定は、現在形を使って表すことができる
Our plane **leaves** Narita for Chicago at 3:30 P.M. tomorrow.
（私たちの飛行機はシカゴに向けて明日の午後3時半に成田を出発します）

**現在進行形** 現在進行形でも確定している未来の予定を表すことができる
**I'm visiting** Taiwan next Monday on a business trip.
（来週月曜日は出張で台湾を訪れます）
*come, go, start, leave, visit, move などの動詞がよく使用されます。

**未来進行形** **未来のある時点で**進行中の動作・出来事を表す
At this time tomorrow, they**'ll be driving** through central London.
（明日の今頃、彼らはロンドンの中心部を車で通過しているだろう）
*「未来のある時点」＝明日の今頃

**未来完了形** 〈**will have ＋過去分詞**〉の形で、**未来のある時点までの**次の3つを表す
**① 完了・結果**
By the time you arrive at the airport, the airplane **will have departed**.
（あなたが空港に到着するまでには、飛行機は出発してしまっているだろう）
*「未来のある時点」＝あなたが空港に到着するとき
**② 経験**
If I visit Thailand again, **I'll have been** there three times.
（もう一度タイに行けば、3回訪れたことになる）
*「未来のある時点」＝もう一度タイを訪れるとき
**③ 継続**
We**'ll have lived** abroad for exactly two years in April.
（4月になれば、私たちはちょうど2年間海外に住んでいることになる）
*「未来のある時点」＝4月

☞時や条件を表す副詞節の中では、たとえ未来のことであっても will を使うことはできません。**現在形**を使用するようにしましょう。
[○] If it **snows** tomorrow morning, I will take a taxi to the station.
[×] If it **will snow** tomorrow morning, I will take a taxi to the station.
（明日の朝雪が降るなら、駅までタクシーで行きます）
ただし、名詞節の中では未来のことを言うときに will を使うことができます。
[○] We have no idea when this bus **will** arrive at our hotel.
（私たちは、このバスがいつホテルに到着するのかわからない）

## Part 5 Incomplete Sentences

***A word or phrase is missing in each of the sentences below. Choose the best word or phrase to complete the sentence.***

**14.** The New Swan Hotel -------- a special discount to frequent guests who book online by the end of the month.
(A) will offer
(B) to offer
(C) offering
(D) is offered
Ⓐ Ⓑ Ⓒ Ⓓ

**15.** In order to accommodate increased numbers of passengers, the airport authority -------- a new terminal building in the next financial year.
(A) to construct
(B) has constructed
(C) constructed
(D) is constructing
Ⓐ Ⓑ Ⓒ Ⓓ

**16.** By the time Ms. Harris arrives at the hotel, our team -------- in the lobby to welcome her and give her the updated itinerary for her trip.
(A) is gathering
(B) will have gathered
(C) had been gathered
(D) to gather
Ⓐ Ⓑ Ⓒ Ⓓ

**17.** Passengers with special dietary needs -------- to indicate this when making their booking online.
(A) have requested
(B) will request
(C) will have requested
(D) are requested
Ⓐ Ⓑ Ⓒ Ⓓ

**18.** According to the timetable on their Web site, the Barrett Mountain tour bus -------- at 8 o'clock tomorrow morning.
(A) departs
(B) has departed
(C) departing
(D) to depart
Ⓐ Ⓑ Ⓒ Ⓓ

**Study Point** Part 6 長文穴埋め問題

このパートはPart 5の長文バージョンです。問題を解く際には、空所のある文だけを読むのではなく、その**前後の文**も読むように心がけましょう。なお、問題形式は**語彙・文法問題**が中心ですが、大問1問の中に、**空所に入る1文を選択する問題**が必ず出されます。その問題を解く際には、**直前の文**が最も重要になります。

[ Question 22 ]
As for public transportation, the subway runs every 30 minutes to Central Square where the hotel is located, at a cost of $12. ---22---

* 下線を引いた文と最も結びつきの強い選択肢をQ22の4つから選びましょう。

## Part 6 Text Completion

***Read a short text. Some words, phrases or sentences are missing from the text. Read the questions and choose the answer to complete the text.***

**Questions 19 to 22** refer to the following e-mail.

To: Ellis Pravadi
From: Donald Faltermeyer
Re: Transportation to the Regal Hotel
Date: 17 July

Thank you for your inquiry regarding transportation from the airport to the Regal Hotel. Unfortunately, our hotel does not offer a ------- **19.** transportation service. However, our team will be glad ------- **20.** a private taxi transfer for you. Please note that there are also ------- **21.** of taxis waiting at the airport, which will cost approximately $80. As for public transportation, the subway runs every 30 minutes to Central Square where the hotel is located, at a cost of $12. ------- **22.** .

**19.** (A) temporary
(B) voluntary
(C) complimentary
(D) solitary
Ⓐ Ⓑ Ⓒ Ⓓ

**20.** (A) to arrange
(B) arranging
(C) arranged
(D) have arranged
Ⓐ Ⓑ Ⓒ Ⓓ

**21.** (A) many
(B) some
(C) plenty
(D) much
Ⓐ Ⓑ Ⓒ Ⓓ

**22.** (A) Make sure to tell the driver that you will be staying at the Regal Hotel.
(B) However, suitcases must be checked in before boarding.
(C) Please send us your transportation fee by bank transfer as soon as possible.
(D) In addition, public bus Number 82 runs frequently to Central Square.
Ⓐ Ⓑ Ⓒ Ⓓ

## Study Point Part 7 読解問題

実際の TOEIC L&R TEST では**時間配分**が重要になります。以下はあくまでも 1 つの目安に過ぎませんが、授業中から常に時間を意識して問題を解いていきましょう。最初のうちは、時間内にすべての問題を解くのは難しいかもしれませんが、続けていくうちに徐々に慣れてくるので、諦めずに最後まで頑張ってください。

| Reading Section (Part 5 – 7) | | 100 問 | 75 分 | 解答時間の目安 |
|---|---|---|---|---|
| Part 5 | 短文穴埋め問題 | 30 問 | 10 分 | 1 問あたり **20 秒** |
| Part 6 | 長文穴埋め問題 | 16 問 | 8 分 | 1 問あたり **30 秒** |
| Part 7 | 1 つの文書 | 29 問 | 29 分 | 1 問あたり **1 分** |
| Part 7 | 複数の文書 | 25 問 | 28 分 | 1 問あたり **1 分＋α** |

## Part 7 Single Passage

***Read the text and the questions following the text. Select the best answer for each question.***

**Questions 23 to 26** refer to the following e-mail.

| | |
|---|---|
| To: | Kelly Hofstede <khofstede@nxtvr.com> |
| From: | Jeffrey Davis <jdavis@nxtvr.com> |
| Subject: | Business trip |
| Date: | August 11 |

Hi, Kelly.

Are you ready for tomorrow?

I just received a call from Lili at Intec Corporation. It seems that Mr. Lee has some urgent business on Thursday morning so she is asking us if we can start the factory tour at an earlier time. I think that's fine, so I have already agreed to the change.

One other thing. Mr. Cheung at Arp Corporation contacted me. He's wondering if we can bring some samples of our new product to show them during the meeting on Friday afternoon. He seems interested, so I think we should do that.

However, it means we'll need to bring another suitcase and we'll go over our weight limit for the flight. Could you handle that change online this afternoon? It's OK to pay more. Many thanks.

Jeffrey

**23.** What is the purpose of the e-mail?
(A) To order some samples
(B) To inquire about a client's availability
(C) To prepare for a business trip
(D) To make reservations for a flight
Ⓐ Ⓑ Ⓒ Ⓓ

**24.** What does Intec Corporation ask to have changed?
(A) The schedule
(B) The location
(C) The transportation method
(D) The accommodation
Ⓐ Ⓑ Ⓒ Ⓓ

**25.** Why did Mr. Cheung contact Mr. Davis?
(A) To arrange a purchase
(B) To make a request
(C) To schedule a delivery
(D) To place an order
Ⓐ Ⓑ Ⓒ Ⓓ

**26.** What does Mr. Davis ask Ms. Hofstede to do?
(A) Choose a different flight
(B) Create some new product samples
(C) Change the departure date
(D) Increase the baggage allowance
Ⓐ Ⓑ Ⓒ Ⓓ

## Review Exercise

***Read this shorter version of the e-mail in Part 7. Fill in appropriate words in the blank spaces from the box below.***

Hi, Kelly.

Lili at Intec Corporation [1]__________ this morning. Mr. Lee is [2]__________ on Thursday morning, so they want us to make the factory tour [3]__________. I already said [4]__________. Also, I got a message from Mr. Cheung. They want to see samples of our latest [5]__________ at our meeting. Let's [6]__________ them, but we'll have to [7]__________ for extra baggage. Could you do that [8]__________?

Jeff

| | | | |
|---|---|---|---|
| (a) earlier | (b) bring | (c) online | (d) product |
| (e) called | (f) pay | (g) yes | (h) busy |

MEMO

UNIT 02

# Meetings and Seminars

## Vocabulary Exercise

*Match each English word with its meaning in Japanese.*

**1.** agenda (　　)　**2.** manufacture (　　)　**3.** enhance (　　)

**4.** in the meantime (　　)　**5.** associate (　　)　**6.** spending (　　)

**7.** reminder (　　)　**8.** crucial (　　)　**9.** on the way (　　)　**10.** mandatory (　　)

a. 極めて重要な　b. 同僚、仕事仲間　c. 高める　d. 製造する　e. 途中で
f. その間に　g. 強制的な、全員参加の　h. 議題　i. 思い出させるもの　j. 経費

# LISTENING SECTION

## Dictation Exercise

*Listen to the following sentences. Fill in the blank spaces.*

1. The projector is ________________ the ceiling, so use this remote control to switch it on.
2. That museum is very interesting. It is well ________________ a look.
3. The back room of the restaurant is private and can ________________12 guests.
4. The president resigned suddenly for ________________ .
5. In the meantime, Ann Harris has been asked to be ________________ president.

**Study Point**　Part 1　写真描写問題

写真に人物が写っていない場合は、音声が流れる前に、次のことを行ってください。

**1.** 写っているものを一通りすべて確認しましょう。
**「何がありますか?」**→ 例）コンピューターとプリンターがある

**2.** 写っているものの**位置関係**や**状態**などに注目しましょう。
**「どこにありますか?」**→ 例）コンピューターとプリンターが**机の上**にある
(There are a computer and a printer on the desk.)

**「どんな位置関係ですか?」**→ 例）プリンターが PC の**隣り**にある
(A printer is next to a computer.)

**「どんな状態ですか?」**→ 例）プリンターがコンピューターに**接続**されている
(A printer is connected to a computer.)

## Part 1 Photographs

***Look at the picture and listen to four statements. Choose one statement that best describes the situation in the picture.***

1.

Ⓐ Ⓑ Ⓒ Ⓓ

2.

Ⓐ Ⓑ Ⓒ Ⓓ

### Study Point Part 2 応答問題

疑問詞 **How** を使用した問いかけにはいくつか種類があります。

1. How **many** employees will participate in the seminar? – Twenty one signed up.
   (そのセミナーには何人の社員が参加する予定ですか)
2. How **long** will we have to wait for a table? – Probably for half an hour.
   (私たちはどのくらいの間、テーブルが空くのを待たなければなりませんか)
3. How **often** does the train stop here? – Every 40 minutes.
   (どのくらいの頻度で電車はここに止まりますか)
4. How **far** in advance should I make my appointment? – A week ahead is good.
   (どれくらい前もって予約をするべきですか)
5. How did you like the movie last night? – I really enjoyed it.
   (昨夜の映画はいかがでしたか)

## Part 2 Question-Response

CD 1-17～21

***Listen to a question or statement and three responses. Choose the best response to the question or statement.***

3. Mark your answer on your answer sheet. (A) (B) (C)
4. Mark your answer on your answer sheet. (A) (B) (C)
5. Mark your answer on your answer sheet. (A) (B) (C)
6. Mark your answer on your answer sheet. (A) (B) (C)
7. Mark your answer on your answer sheet. (A) (B) (C)

### Study Point　Part 3　会話問題

設問の中に図表がある場合は、音声が流れる前に、英文だけでなくその図表の内容も頭に入れておきましょう。そして、どんな内容の英文が読み上げられるのか想像してみましょう。以下に具体的なものを示しておきます。

**図表の具体例：**

- 割引率が記載されたクーポン
- 列車の時刻表
- 店舗の位置を示す地図
- 商品の価格表
- レストランのメニュー
- ビルのフロア案内
- 展示会場の間取り図
- 社内研修の日程表
- 会議の議題と時間
- 会議室の収容人数
- 月毎の売上高を示した棒グラフ

## Part 3 Conversation

***Listen to a conversation between two people. Read the questions on your answer sheet. Choose the best answer for each question.***

8. According to the woman, what has changed about the project meeting?
   (A) The number of participants
   (B) The date
   (C) The start time
   (D) The meeting agenda
   (A) (B) (C) (D)

9. Look at the graphic. Which room will probably be used?
   (A) Room 102
   (B) Room 107
   (C) Room 203
   (D) Room 301
   (A) (B) (C) (D)

10. What does the man ask the woman to do?
   (A) Order some refreshments
   (B) Share new information
   (C) Cancel a meeting
   (D) Conduct a training workshop
   (A) (B) (C) (D)

| Meeting Room | Capacity |
|---|---|
| Room 102 | Up to 6 people |
| Room 107 | Up to 24 people |
| Room 203 | Up to 12 people |
| Room 301 | Up to 4 people |

## Study Point　Part 4 説明文問題

このパートでは会社名や人名、地名などがよく登場します。これらは聞き慣れないものも多いため、受験生を混乱させる原因の1つとなっています。設問や選択肢の中に固有名詞を見つけたら、頭の中で発音して準備をしましょう。

例 1）What did **ComTrek** do in April?
→ トークの中に **ComTrek** という会社名が登場します。

例 2）Why does the speaker congratulate **Novio Esqueda**?
→ トークの中に **Novio Esqueda** という名前の人物が登場します。

例 3）Why is the group traveling to **Teraville**?
→ トークの中に **Teraville**（サウスダコタ州の町）という地名が登場します。

## Part 4 Talk

***Listen to a talk given by a single speaker. Read the questions on your answer sheet. Choose the best answer for each question.***

**11.** What is the main topic of the meeting?
(A) A company policy
(B) An upcoming position
(C) A newly hired associate
(D) A project delay
Ⓐ Ⓑ Ⓒ Ⓓ

**12.** What does the speaker mean when he says, "but he can't do everything"?
(A) Mr. Sunderland does not know how to do all his jobs.
(B) Mr. Sunderland has little time for all his work.
(C) Mr. Sunderland is considering starting his own company.
(D) Mr. Sunderland is a new employee.
Ⓐ Ⓑ Ⓒ Ⓓ

**13.** What department does Mr. Sunderland work in?
(A) Accounting
(B) IT
(C) Human Resources
(D) Marketing
Ⓐ Ⓑ Ⓒ Ⓓ

# READING SECTION

## Study Point Part 5 短文穴埋め問題

### 現在分詞／過去分詞

**現在分詞**

**1. 自動詞**

Long-term labor contracts are not so common in **developing** countries.
（長期雇用契約は、発展途上国ではそんなに一般的ではない）

*自動詞の現在分詞は**「～している」**という**進行中の動作**を表します。ちなみに、**developed** countries は「（発展した国→）先進国」を意味します。詳しくは、以下の **過去分詞** **1. 自動詞** を参照して下さい。

**2. 他動詞**

It is an **astonishing** achievement to lead the team to victory.
（そのチームを勝利に導いたのは驚くべき功績だ）

*「驚かす」や「悩ます」といった**感情に影響を与えるような他動詞**の現在分詞は、「（人を）～させる」という**能動**の意味を持ちます。astonishing は「（人を驚かせる→）驚くべき」の意味になります。

**過去分詞**

**1. 自動詞**

A **retired** police officer was invited as a guest speaker to the seminar.
（ある**退職した**警察官が、ゲストスピーカーとしてそのセミナーに招かれた）

*自動詞の過去分詞は**「～した、～してしまった」**という**結果・完了**の状態を表します。**「～される」**という**受動**の意味にはなりません。その他に、**failed** project（失敗したプロジェクト）や **advanced** technology（高度の科学技術）も紹介しておきます。

**2. 他動詞**

The passengers patiently waited for the **delayed** train.
（その乗客たちは**遅れている**電車を辛抱強く待っていた）

*他動詞の過去分詞は**「～された」**という**受動**の意味を表します。delay は「～を遅らせる」という意味の他動詞なので、delayed は「（遅らせられた→）遅れた」となります。ここで delaying は誤りです。その他に、**trusted** recipe（信頼できるレシピ）や **celebrated** author（著名な [←世に知られている] 作者）も確認しておきましょう。

**間違いやすい例**

A. It was an **exciting** game from start to finish.
（それは最初から最後までわくわくさせるような試合だった）

B. The **excited** supporters did not leave the stadium after the game was over.
（興奮したサポーターたちは、試合が終わってもスタジアムを去らなかった）

*excite は「（人を）興奮させる」という意味の他動詞なので、exciting は「（興奮させる→）わくわくさせるような」という**能動**の意味で、excited は「（興奮させられた→）興奮した」という**受動**の意味を持ちます。

## Part 5 Incomplete Sentences

***A word or phrase is missing in each of the sentences below. Choose the best word or phrase to complete the sentence.***

**14.** At the meeting, ARC Auto decided to manufacture a ------- version of its entry-level truck.
(A) modernize
(B) modernizing
(C) modernized
(D) modernization
Ⓐ Ⓑ Ⓒ Ⓓ

**15.** Organizing online meetings with staff in various countries is a -------- aspect of Ms. Blake's job.
(A) challenge
(B) challenges
(C) challenged
(D) challenging
Ⓐ Ⓑ Ⓒ Ⓓ

**16.** Before the meeting last week, participants ------- their budget requests.
(A) submitted
(B) submitting
(C) submit
(D) submission
Ⓐ Ⓑ Ⓒ Ⓓ

**17.** Although Ms. Prasad had a long and -------- journey, she was on time for the meeting.
(A) tire
(B) tiring
(C) tired
(D) tires
Ⓐ Ⓑ Ⓒ Ⓓ

**18.** The start time of the ------- meeting about the budget will be 4:00 P.M.
(A) delay
(B) delays
(C) delayed
(D) delaying
Ⓐ Ⓑ Ⓒ Ⓓ

**Study Point** Part 6 長文穴埋め問題

Part 4と同様に、このパートでも次のような指示文が登場します。
Questions 19 to 22 refer to the following **memo**.
（メモ）
ここでも下線部分は文書の内容によって異なるため、安易に見逃さず、どんな文書なのかを理解した上で読み進めていくことをお勧めします。以下のものがよく登場します。

***letter*** (手紙) / ***e-mail*** (Eメール) / ***article*** (記事) / ***notice*** (お知らせ) / ***advertisement*** (広告) / ***information*** (案内) / ***press release*** (プレスリリース) / ***instructions*** (指示) / ***recipe*** (レシピ) / ***review*** (レビュー) / ***brochure*** (パンフレット) / ***job listing*** (求人情報) / ***excerpt from a guidebook*** (ガイドブックからの抜粋)

## Part 6 Text Completion

***Read a short text. Some words, phrases or sentences are missing from the text. Read the questions and choose the answer to complete the text.***

**Questions 19 to 22** refer to the following memo.

**MEMO**

To: All Staff
From: Jenny Marr, General Affairs Department
Subject: Meeting on New Office Procedures
Date: 7 January, 2024

We are introducing new office procedures that ------- (**19.**) our workflow, efficiency, and overall office environment. To ------- (**20.**) a smooth transition and understanding of these changes, we have scheduled a mandatory meeting for all staff members.

Meeting Details:
Date: 15 January, 2024
Time: 10:00 A.M.
Location: Conference Room A

Your attendance is crucial ------- (**21.**) these procedures will impact all departments. Please mark your calendars and make the necessary arrangements to be present. ------- (**22.**) .

Thank you for your attention to this matter.

**19.** (A) to enhance
(B) are enhanced
(C) will enhance
(D) had been enhanced
Ⓐ Ⓑ Ⓒ Ⓓ

**20.** (A) ensure
(B) finalize
(C) clarify
(D) inform
Ⓐ Ⓑ Ⓒ Ⓓ

**21.** (A) if
(B) as
(C) to
(D) on
Ⓐ Ⓑ Ⓒ Ⓓ

**22.** (A) When you have decided whether to attend or not, please contact Jenny Marr (ext. 2066).
(B) If you have any questions or concerns, please reach out to Jenny Marr (ext. 2066).
(C) Jenny Marr (ext. 2066) will contact you later to let you know the meeting details.
(D) Your idea for a new office procedure should be submitted to Jenny Marr (ext. 2066).
Ⓐ Ⓑ Ⓒ Ⓓ

**Study Point** Part 7 読解問題

このパートでも次のような指示文が登場します。Part 7は他のパートよりも多様な表現が使用されるので、数多く紹介します。

Questions 23 to 26 refer to the following **online discussion**.
（オンラインチャットの話し合い）

***schedule*** （スケジュール） / ***agenda*** （議題、進行表） / ***order form*** （注文用紙） / ***profile*** （プロフィール） / ***coupon*** （クーポン） / ***receipt*** （領収書） / ***credit card statement*** （クレジットカード明細書） / ***flyer*** （チラシ） / ***invitation*** （招待状） / ***online post*** （オンラインの投稿） / ***invoice*** （請求書） / ***product usage instructions*** （製品使用説明書） / ***packing slip*** （梱包票） / ***online customer service exchange*** （オンライン顧客サービスのやりとり） / ***customer reviews*** （顧客レビュー） / ***tracking information*** （追跡情報） / ***certificate*** （証明書） / ***resume*** （経歴書） / ***cost estimate*** （費用見積書） / ***editor's note*** （編集後記） / ***expense report*** （経費報告書） / ***job summaries*** （職務概要） / ***text-message chain*** （テキストメッセージのやりとり）

## Part 7 Single Passage

***Read the text and the questions following the text. Select the best answer for each question.***

**Questions 23 to 26** refer to the following online discussion.

**Andy Marquez (9:04 A.M.)**
Is everybody ready for the meeting? Remember, this one is important. If we can persuade TechStar to purchase our new products, we could get a lot of new business from other companies, too.

**Susan Littleton (9:06 A.M.)**
I think we're all good. I've got the new samples packed safely in a small case. Mark, how about the presentation?

**Mark Adeoye (9:09 A.M.)**
The slideshow is all done. I updated the pricing information based on Andy's e-mail of the day before yesterday, although I haven't indicated any information about possible discounts.

**Andy Marquez (9:12 A.M.)**
No, that's fine. It's too early to make any promises yet, but during the meeting I can give a general indication of the kind of discounts we can offer.

**Mark Adeoye (9:14 A.M.)**
By the way, how long do you think this will last? I need to be back in the office by 3:00.

**Andy Marquez (9:15 A.M.)**
Well, the meeting is scheduled for 11:00 to 1:00. Susan, what do you think? You're driving us there and back.

**Susan Littleton (9:17 A.M.)**
I've visited companies in the Hampton Industrial Park before. It only takes about 30 minutes to get there, even if the traffic is heavy. You'll be fine, Mark.

**Mark Adeoye (9:18 A.M.)**
Thanks. Glad to know that.

**Andy Marquez (9:20 A.M.)**
Great. Anyway, I will see you both down in the lobby in about 20 minutes. An early start will give us time to grab a coffee and bagel on the way.

**23.** Who most likely are the writers?
(A) Accounts staff
(B) Sales staff
(C) Purchasing staff
(D) Human Resources staff

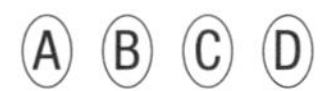
Ⓐ Ⓑ Ⓒ Ⓓ

**24.** At 9:06 A.M., what does Ms. Littleton mean when she writes, "I think we're all good"?
(A) The preparations are complete.
(B) All the new products are excellent.
(C) New business would be welcome.
(D) Other companies are acceptable, too.

Ⓐ Ⓑ Ⓒ Ⓓ

**25.** What is indicated about Mr. Marquez?
(A) He packed the samples himself.
(B) He will leave the discounting decisions to Mr. Adeoye.
(C) He cannot promise that he will attend the meeting.
(D) He contacted Mr. Adeoye earlier this week.

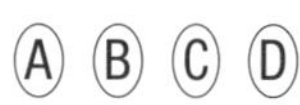
Ⓐ Ⓑ Ⓒ Ⓓ

**26.** Why does Mr. Marquez want to make an early start?
(A) To discuss the meeting agenda
(B) To avoid heavy traffic on the way
(C) To get some refreshments
(D) To hold a meeting in the lobby

Ⓐ Ⓑ Ⓒ Ⓓ

## Review Exercise

***Read this summary of the online discussion in Part 7. Fill in appropriate words in the blank spaces from the box below.***

Andy Marquez is [1]__________ that two other staff members are ready for the meeting with clients. Susan Littleton will [2]__________ the product samples, and Mark Adeoye is in [3]________ of the presentation. Both of them are ready, [4]________ there is no information about discounts in the presentation slideshow. Mr. Marquez says that it is no [5]________. Mr. Adeoye has to [6]________ to the office for an afternoon meeting. Ms. Littleton, who is driving today, confirms that he can get back [7]________. They will [8]________ coffee and bagels on the way to the meeting.

| | | | |
|---|---|---|---|
| (a) charge | (b) return | (c) checking | (d) in time |
| (e) although | (f) buy | (g) problem | (h) bring |

MEMO

UNIT 03

# Restaurants

## Vocabulary Exercise

*Match each English word with its meaning in Japanese.*

**1.** recipe (　　) **2.** bill (　　) **3.** stack (　　) **4.** occasionally (　　)
**5.** tip (　　) **6.** diner (　　) **7.** server (　　) **8.** renovate (　　)
**9.** complimentary (　　) **10.** branch (　　)

a. 支店　b. 食事客　c. チップを渡す　d. 時折　e. 無料の
f. 請求金額、請求書　g. 積み上げる　h. 改装する　i. レシピ　j. 給仕係

# LISTENING SECTION

## Dictation Exercise

1-26

*Listen to the following sentences. Fill in the blank spaces.*

1. That new ________________ apartment building has blocked our view of the mountains.
2. Employees at Gerton Corporation can take their paid leave ________________ they want.
3. Many people are ________________ to pollen, and suffer various symptoms in the spring.
4. Amanda went ________________ to make us feel welcome at the party.
5. Our holiday to Paris was ________________ , mainly thanks to the amazing food.

**Study Point** Part 1 写真描写問題

写真に3人以上の人物が写っている場合は、まず①**その中で1番目立つ人に注目しましょう。**その後、②**残りの人たちの間に共通点**があるかどうか確認しましょう。

左の写真の場合、以下のどちらかが正解になる可能性があります。

1. 最も目立つ人物に関する描写
   A man is cutting meat with a knife.
2. 残りの人たちの共通点に関する描写
   They're watching how to cut meat.

## Part 1 Photographs

1-27, 28

***Look at the picture and listen to four statements. Choose one statement that best describes the situation in the picture.***

1.

Ⓐ Ⓑ Ⓒ Ⓓ

2.

Ⓐ Ⓑ Ⓒ Ⓓ

### Study Point Part 2 応答問題

最初に読まれる文章が疑問文ではなく、肯定文であることも少なくありません。その中には、肯定文の文末に **right?** を付けて「～ですよね?」と確認する形も存在します。

**Q1.** Your shop is moving to a new location, **right?**
(あなたの店は新しい場所に移転するのですよね?)
**A1.** Yes, we've been packing all week.

**Q2.** I can recycle this plastic bottle, **right?**
(このペットボトルはリサイクルできるのですよね?)
**A2.** Correct, so please put it in that bin.

**Q3.** This train stops at South Street, **right?**
(この電車はサウス・ストリート駅に止まりますよね?)
**A3.** You'll need to transfer at Union Station.

## Part 2 Question-Response

1-29~33

***Listen to a question or statement and three responses. Choose the best response to the question or statement.***

3. Mark your answer on your answer sheet. Ⓐ Ⓑ Ⓒ

4. Mark your answer on your answer sheet. Ⓐ Ⓑ Ⓒ

5. Mark your answer on your answer sheet. Ⓐ Ⓑ Ⓒ

6. Mark your answer on your answer sheet. Ⓐ Ⓑ Ⓒ

7. Mark your answer on your answer sheet. Ⓐ Ⓑ Ⓒ

### Study Point Part 3 会話問題

Part 3とPart 4では、**話し手の意図を問う**問題も出されます。限られた時間ではありますが、まずは音声が流れる前に、その質問があるかどうかを確認し、引用されている文の内容を把握しましょう。そして、会話全体を理解する手掛かりにもなるので、しっかり記憶しておきましょう。

例) What does the man mean when he says, "**I helped Alex fix his webcam last week**"?
この部分に注目です。

## Part 3 Conversation

1-34, 35

***Listen to a conversation between two people. Read the questions on your answer sheet. Choose the best answer for each question.***

8. Why is the woman calling?
   (A) To change an appointment
   (B) To request more information
   (C) To inquire about food items
   (D) To make a reservation
   Ⓐ Ⓑ Ⓒ Ⓓ

9. What is the woman concerned about?
   (A) The cost of soy products
   (B) Her husband's food allergy
   (C) How she can access the location
   (D) The opening and closing times
   Ⓐ Ⓑ Ⓒ Ⓓ

10. What does the man mean when he says, "please be sure to remind your server when you order"?
   (A) He hopes the woman does not forget her order.
   (B) He suggests the woman tell the server about the special request.
   (C) He thinks the woman might forget who her server is.
   (D) He wants the woman to remember to tip the server.
   Ⓐ Ⓑ Ⓒ Ⓓ

**Study Point** Part 4 説明文問題

Part 4では、1つのトークに対して3つ質問されます。基本的に、第1問目は **Who most likely is the speaker?**（話し手は誰だと考えられますか）や **What is the topic of the talk?**（トークのテーマは何ですか）といった**概要**に関するもので、それ以降は**内容に関する**細かい質問が続きます。話の流れに沿って質問されるので、例外があるかもしれませんが、おおよそ次のような構成になっていると考えてよいでしょう。

**第1問**：概要に関する設問　→　トーク全体の**前半**部分に注目
**第2問**：細かい内容に関する設問　→　トーク全体の**中盤**部分に注目
**第3問**：細かい内容に関する設問　→　トーク全体の**後半**部分に注目

## Part 4 Talk

***Listen to a talk given by a single speaker. Read the questions on your answer sheet. Choose the best answer for each question.***

**11.** Who most likely is the speaker?
(A) A food reviewer
(B) A pastry chef
(C) A restaurant owner
(D) A server
Ⓐ Ⓑ Ⓒ Ⓓ

**12.** What does the speaker mean when she says, "The chef goes out of his way to make it unforgettable"?
(A) The chef has a unique technique with chicken.
(B) The chef sometimes forgets the menu items.
(C) The chef uses his own personal recipes.
(D) The chef works hard to create a memorable dish.
Ⓐ Ⓑ Ⓒ Ⓓ

**13.** What does the speaker say she will do next?
(A) Ask the chef a question
(B) Bring a free item
(C) Calculate the bill
(D) Describe a new dish
Ⓐ Ⓑ Ⓒ Ⓓ

# READING SECTION

**Study Point** Part 5 短文穴埋め問題

## 代名詞

1. ① **those who** ... = (the) people who ...「～する人々」
   This restaurant is good for **those who** have food allergies.
   (このレストランは食物アレルギーがある人たちにおすすめだ)
   ② **anyone who** ... = any people who ... / whoever ...「～する人は誰でも」
   We offer a 10% discount on food to **anyone who** is over 60.
   (60 歳以上の方には誰にでも 10%割引で食事を提供します)
   *those の代わりに anyone を使うと「誰でも」の部分が強調されます。また、those who は**複数扱い**ですが、anyone who は**単数扱い**になります。

2. ① **that of** (前に出た名詞が**単数形**の場合に使用する)
   The population of Japan is almost the same as **that of** Mexico.
   (日本の人口はメキシコの人口とほぼ同じだ) *that = the population
   ② **those of** (前に出た名詞が**複数形**の場合に使用する)
   Raw foods especially **those of** animal origin must be properly cooked.
   (生もの、特に動物性のものは適切に調理しなければならない) * those = raw foods

3. ① **one**
   I want a new smartphone, but I don't have enough money to buy **one**.
   (新しいスマホが欲しいけれど、買うのに十分なお金がない) *one = a smartphone
   *one は「(同じ種類の) **不特定**の 1 つのもの」を意味していて、名詞の繰り返しを避けるために使用されます。
   ② **the one**
   Of all the dishes on the menu, **the one** most people order is Margherita pizza. *the one = the dish
   (メニューにあるすべての料理のうち、最も多くの人が注文するのはマルゲリータピザだ)
   *one の前に the が付くことで「**特定**の (～な) もの」という意味になります。

4. ① **both of ～**「(2 つ [ 人 ] のうちの) どちらも」 * 複数扱い
   **Both of** my children like junk food. (私の子供たちはどちらもジャンクフードが好きだ)
   ② **either of ～**「(2 つ [ 人 ] のうちの) どちらか一方、どちらでも」 * 単数扱い
   You can choose **either of** the following two methods. (次の 2 つの手段のどちらか一方を選べます)
   ③ **each of ～**「(2 つ [ 人 ] 以上のうちの) それぞれが」 * 単数扱い
   **Each of** these products is made in Japan. (これらの製品はそれぞれ日本製だ)
   ④ **neither of ～**「(2 つ [ 人 ] のうちの) どちらも～ない」 * 通常は単数扱い (複数も可)
   **Neither of** us agrees with his plan. (私たちのどちらも彼の計画には賛成していない)
   ⑤ **none of ～**「(3 つ [ 人 ] 以上のうちで) どれ [ 誰 ] も～ない」 * 単数・複数両方可
   **None of** the students failed the exam.(その試験に落ちた学生は一人もいなかった)

## Part 5 Incomplete Sentences

***A word or phrase is missing in each of the sentences below. Choose the best word or phrase to complete the sentence.***

**14.** The décor inside the restaurant will be familiar for -------- who has visited Morocco before.
(A) those
(B) there
(C) anyone
(D) customers
Ⓐ Ⓑ Ⓒ Ⓓ

**15.** The quality of the food at The Green Garden is comparable to -------- of a 5-star hotel's kitchen.
(A) that
(B) those
(C) this
(D) these
Ⓐ Ⓑ Ⓒ Ⓓ

**16.** Although Mr. Davis said that he wanted a dessert, he had difficulty choosing -------- because they all looked so delicious.
(A) one
(B) the one
(C) one's
(D) in one
Ⓐ Ⓑ Ⓒ Ⓓ

**17.** For this set course, there are only two options for the side dish, but -------- of the two will definitely be good.
(A) those
(B) either
(C) also
(D) together
Ⓐ Ⓑ Ⓒ Ⓓ

**18.** -------- of the three restaurants inside the hotel seemed appealing, so we chose to eat at a local restaurant in the downtown area.
(A) Nothing
(B) Not
(C) Neither
(D) None
Ⓐ Ⓑ Ⓒ Ⓓ

### Study Point Part 6 長文穴埋め問題

このパートの設問は、**語彙・文法問題**と**空所に入る1文を選択する問題**の2種類からなりますが、すべての問題が文脈を理解しないと解けないわけではありません。中には、以下のような**品詞や前置詞などを選ぶ問題**があり、それらは空所のある文だけを読めば解くことが可能です。時間がないときは優先して解答しましょう。

**例1）** Long flights can often result in a phenomenon ( known ) as jet lag.
**例2）** I am available Monday ( through ) Friday from 10:00 A.M. to 6:00 P.M.
**例3）** Garbage is collected on ( different ) days depending on your address.

## Part 6 Text Completion

***Read a short text. Some words, phrases or sentences are missing from the text. Read the questions and choose the answer to complete the text.***

**Questions 19 to 22** refer to the following article.

**Local Bakery Has Big Plans**

When Jenny Adams started selling freshly baked bagels from her home in Kendalwood, she wasn't sure if her small business would be a -------(**19.**) . But now, 15 years later, she has become the proud owner of Adams' Bagels and Coffee, which is -------(**20.**) in South Kendalwood Shopping Mall.
On a busy Saturday morning, we saw a line of people waiting to enter the café, with many saying that they come every week. "All our bagels are still freshly baked by us," said Jenny, "although these days we have our own baking -------(**21.**) . My kitchen got too small!"
And now the business is looking to expand. -------(**22.**) .

**19.** (A) success
(B) successful
(C) successfully
(D) successive
Ⓐ Ⓑ Ⓒ Ⓓ

**20.** (A) location
(B) located
(C) locating
(D) locates
Ⓐ Ⓑ Ⓒ Ⓓ

**21.** (A) quantity
(B) utility
(C) facility
(D) priority
Ⓐ Ⓑ Ⓒ Ⓓ

**22.** (A) Customers who visit next Saturday will each receive a 20 percent discount.
(B) The interior décor will be renovated in a Mediterranean style.
(C) A second branch is scheduled to open in Mapleville later this year.
(D) The top-selling item on the menu is the Blueberry Bagel and Coffee set.
Ⓐ Ⓑ Ⓒ Ⓓ

**Study Point** Part 7 読解問題

このパートでは英文の内容に関する問題が中心となりますが、同義語を選ぶ問題が出される場合もあります。次のような聞き方をしますので、使用されている語の意味もしっかり理解しておきましょう。

例）The word “meet” in **paragraph** 3, **line** 4, is closest in meaning to
（第 3 段落 4 行目にある “meet” に最も意味が近いのは ...）
(A) connect
(B) present
(C) satisfy
(D) encounter

*__paragraph__：段落　**line**：行

## Part 7 Single Passage

***Read the text and the questions following the text. Select the best answer for each question.***

**Questions 23 to 26** refer to the following Web page.

https: //saltsprayrestaurant.us

| Home | Menu | About Us | Access |
|---|---|---|---|

**The Salt Spray Seafood Restaurant**

Our Philosophy:
All fish served in our restaurant are locally caught, either by ourselves or by our friends. As part of the local fishing community, we aim to supply sustainable seafood and protect our beautiful oceans.

Our History:
Our first restaurant was established on Eastside Dock in 1978. Since then, we have grown bigger and moved to a new location in the Bayside Marina. We are a family-owned business, with three generations of our family currently working in our restaurant.

Our Menu:
While not large, our menu offers delicious and carefully selected fish dishes, from cod and chips to a whole lobster plate, with specials depending on the fish caught on the day. Click on the following link to see today’s specials.
Today’s Specials → https://saltsprayrestaurant.us/specials

Customers at The Salt Spray can choose seating either indoors or outdoors, and we accept telephone orders for pickup. Delivery is not available. Child seats available on request. Please understand that, due to high demand, we do not take reservations.

Sign up to join our mailing list:
Just access the form below and fill out your details to sign up. You will receive news of special dishes and special discounts every week. We also occasionally offer fishing tours accompanied by our staff—check the mails regularly for more information.
Newsletter Sign Up → https://saltsprayrestaurant.us/signup

Opening Hours:
Breakfast: Daily From 8:00 A.M. to 10:30 A.M.
Lunch: Daily 11:00 A.M. to 3:30 P.M.
Dinner: Daily 5:00 P.M. to 10:00 P.M. (last orders 9:30 P.M.)

**23.** What is indicated about The Salt Spray Seafood Restaurant?
(A) It donates money to protect the ocean environment.
(B) The owners are also fishermen themselves.
(C) Their fish is supplied from all over the country.
(D) The local fishing community are its main customers.

Ⓐ Ⓑ Ⓒ Ⓓ

**24.** The word "currently" in paragraph 2, line 4, is closest in meaning to
(A) at present
(B) recently
(C) regularly
(D) in cooperation

Ⓐ Ⓑ Ⓒ Ⓓ

**25.** According to the Web page, what is not available?
(A) Dining outside
(B) Self pickup
(C) Seats for children
(D) Table reservations

Ⓐ Ⓑ Ⓒ Ⓓ

**26.** How can customers get information about fishing tours?
(A) By filling out a questionnaire
(B) By picking up a newsletter in the restaurant
(C) By sending an e-mail to the restaurant
(D) By registering online

Ⓐ Ⓑ Ⓒ Ⓓ

## Review Exercise

***Read this shorter version of the Web page in Part 7. Fill in appropriate words in the blank spaces from the box below.***

We catch the fish served in our restaurants [1]__________, in an environmentally friendly way. Our restaurant first opened in 1978, but we are bigger now and have [2]__________ to a new location. We have a carefully [3]__________ menu that focuses on popular dishes, and we also serve different [4]__________ each day. As we have a lot of customers visiting each day, we do not take [5]__________. Please join our mailing list to get news, [6]__________ and more. [7]__________ is easy via our Web site. You can also check our [8]__________ times on the Web site.

| | | | |
|---|---|---|---|
| (a) chosen | (b) discounts | (c) opening | (d) reservations |
| (e) registration | (f) ourselves | (g) specials | (h) moved |

MEMO

UNIT 04

# Company Recruitment

## Vocabulary Exercise

*Match each English word with its meaning in Japanese.*

**1.** personnel (= human resources) department (　　)　**2.** enclosed (　　)
**3.** bachelor's degree (　　)　**4.** gratitude (　　)　**5.** keep in touch (　　)
**6.** applicant (　　)　**7.** contract (　　)　**8.** qualified (　　)
**9.** sign up for (　　)　**10.** orientation (　　)

a. 契約（書）　b. 応募者　c. 同封した　d. 人事部　e. 学士号
f. 申し込む、参加する　g. 資格要件を満たした　h. 新人研修、説明会　i. 感謝の念
j. 連絡を取り合う

# LISTENING SECTION

## Dictation Exercise

*Listen to the following sentences. Fill in the blank spaces.*

1. If you have any questions, please let me know by ____________ your hand.
2. Keep all your receipts from the business trip. You will be reimbursed for ____________ later.
3. My company usually ____________ new staff in the spring.
4. Let's ____________ some pictures on the Web site.
5. My salary is paid by an automatic ____________ directly into my bank account.

**Study Point** Part 1 写真描写問題

物が主語になる場合は受動態がよく使われます。その場合は〈**be 動詞+過去分詞**〉「～される」の受動態なのか、あるいは〈**be 動詞+ being +過去分詞**〉「～されているところだ」という現在進行形の受動態なのかを区別する必要があります。

1. Clothes **are displayed.**
（服が陳列されています）［状態］

2. Clothes **are being displayed.**
（服が陳列されているところです）［動作］

## Part 1 Photographs

CD 1-39, 40

***Look at the picture and listen to four statements. Choose one statement that best describes the situation in the picture.***

1.

Ⓐ Ⓑ Ⓒ Ⓓ

2.

Ⓐ Ⓑ Ⓒ Ⓓ

### Study Point Part 2 応答問題

問いかけで使われている語（句）が選択肢の中に出てくる場合、その選択肢は不正解の可能性があります。（もちろん正解のケースもあります。）自分の答えに確信が持てない限り、そのような選択肢は避けた方が無難かもしれません。

**例）**

問いかけ：Did you participate in that **convention**?（その会議に参加しましたか）

誤答：A **convention** about electronics.（電子機器に関する会議です）

正答：One of my colleagues did.（私の同僚の一人が参加しました）

## Part 2 Question-Response

CD 1-41〜45

***Listen to a question or statement and three responses. Choose the best response to the question or statement.***

3. Mark your answer on your answer sheet. Ⓐ Ⓑ Ⓒ
4. Mark your answer on your answer sheet. Ⓐ Ⓑ Ⓒ
5. Mark your answer on your answer sheet. Ⓐ Ⓑ Ⓒ
6. Mark your answer on your answer sheet. Ⓐ Ⓑ Ⓒ
7. Mark your answer on your answer sheet. Ⓐ Ⓑ Ⓒ

**Study Point** Part 3 会話問題

このパートでは2人または3人の会話が流れますが、特に2人の場合（そのときは自動的に男性1人と女性1人の会話になります）、質問や選択肢の中に the man / the woman / the speakers 以外の人の名前などないでしょうか。もしあれば、2人の会話の中に第三者の話題が出る可能性があります。心の準備をしておきましょう。

例）When will the woman contact **Mr. Park**?
→（2人の会話であれば）女性の方がこの後 **Park さん**に連絡をとることがわかります。

## Part 3 Conversation

1-46, 47

***Listen to a conversation between two people. Read the questions on your answer sheet. Choose the best answer for each question.***

8. What are the speakers discussing?
(A) The price of a product
(B) A staff issue
(C) Store hours
(D) Store location
Ⓐ Ⓑ Ⓒ Ⓓ

9. What happened at the speakers' business last summer?
(A) It introduced a new product that was very popular.
(B) It started targeting tourists for the first time.
(C) There was a sharp increase in customers.
(D) There were many new employees in the summer.
Ⓐ Ⓑ Ⓒ Ⓓ

10. What does the woman imply about Thomas?
(A) He is a good salesperson.
(B) He is familiar with social media.
(C) He was hired last summer.
(D) He was promoted recently.
Ⓐ Ⓑ Ⓒ Ⓓ

## Study Point　Part 4 説明文問題

このパートに登場するトークの種類はさまざまですが、それぞれに一般的な形があります。例えば、**留守番電話のメッセージ**（telephone message）は次のような流れが基本です。

**1.** 自己紹介
例）Hello, this is Lisa Prescott from Davis Medical Clinic.

**2.** 電話をした目的
例）I'm calling about your appointment with Dr. Hall for this Wednesday.

**3.** 追加の説明・情報
例）Unfortunately, he has a conference in New York on that day, and he can't come back until Thursday.

**4.** お願いしたいこと
例）Would you mind changing the date of your appointment?
（予約の日を変更していただけませんか）
Please call us back as soon as possible.

## Part 4 Talk

***Listen to a talk given by a single speaker. Read the questions on your answer sheet. Choose the best answer for each question.***

**11.** Where does the speaker most likely work?
(A) Research and Development
(B) Human Resources
(C) Marketing
(D) Sales
Ⓐ Ⓑ Ⓒ Ⓓ

**12.** What does the speaker ask the listener to do?
(A) Ask his supervisor for some information
(B) Conduct interviews for job candidates
(C) Give a new employee orientation talk
(D) Ask his worker to submit a form
Ⓐ Ⓑ Ⓒ Ⓓ

**13.** What does the speaker want to do by the end of the workday?
(A) Complete a bank procedure
(B) Finish a report
(C) Interview candidates
(D) Meet with a coworker
Ⓐ Ⓑ Ⓒ Ⓓ

# READING SECTION

## Study Point Part 5 短文穴埋め問題

### to 不定詞／動名詞

**to 不定詞の 3 つの用法**

① I would like **to work** in the accounting department of a major publishing house. [ 名詞的 ] （私は大手出版社の経理部で働きたい）

② He is looking for someone **to help** him translate a letter into Japanese. [ 形容詞的 ] （彼は手紙を日本語に翻訳するのを手伝ってくれる人を探している）

③ They went to the library **to prepare** for the final exam. [ 副詞的 ]
（彼らは期末試験の準備をするために図書館に行った）
* ここでは**目的「～するために」**の意味で使われています。この他に、**結果「～した結果…」**、**判断の根拠「～するとは」**、**感情の原因「～して」**、**条件「もし～すれば」**があります。

**動名詞の意味上の主語**

① My father doesn't like **buying** books from online bookstores.
（私の父はオンライン書店で本を買うのが好きではない）

② My father doesn't like **my buying** books from online bookstores.
（私の父は、私がオンライン書店で本を買うのが好きではない）
* 動名詞 **buying** の前に置かれた所有格の代名詞 **my** が意味上の主語です。my buying books で「私が本を買うこと」という意味になるのに対し、動名詞の意味上の主語がない①の文では、本を買うのは「私の父」になります。

**to 不定詞と動名詞の使い分け**

・**to 不定詞だけを目的語にとる動詞**
[ hope / decide / expect / wish / agree / pretend / claim / plan など ]
○ We agreed **to keep** in touch. ✕ We agreed **keeping** in touch.

・**動名詞だけを目的語にとる動詞**
[ enjoy / avoid / consider / admit / recommend / finish / mind / suggest など ]
○ He suggested **taking** a break. ✕ He suggested **to take** a break.

**to 不定詞と動名詞で意味が異なる動詞**

A. to 不定詞は**「未完了のこと」**を表し、動名詞は**「完了したこと」**を表す

① Please remember **to send** me the e-mail. （私にメールを送るのを覚えていて下さい）

② Do you remember **sending** me the e-mail? （私にメールを送ったのを覚えていますか）
*remember の他に forget や regret（後悔する）、try も動名詞と to 不定詞で意味が異なります。

B. to 不定詞は**能動**の意味、そして動名詞は**受動**の意味を表す

① You need **to clean** your room before you leave. （出発前に部屋の掃除が必要だ）

② Your room needs **cleaning** before you leave. = Your room needs **to be cleaned** before you leave.
*need の他に want や deserve（価値がある）も同様の扱いになります。

## Part 5 Incomplete Sentences

***A word or phrase is missing in each of the sentences below. Choose the best word or phrase to complete the sentence.***

**14.** Far Horizon Airlines is hiring new recruits -------- the number of flight attendants on its domestic routes.
(A) increasing
(B) to increase
(C) increased
(D) increase
Ⓐ Ⓑ Ⓒ Ⓓ

**15.** Recruitment advisors do not recommend -------- answers for standard interview questions.
(A) memorizing
(B) to memorize
(C) memorized
(D) memorize
Ⓐ Ⓑ Ⓒ Ⓓ

**16.** Although HayTech Media was expected -------- eight new recruits, only five candidates submitted their applications.
(A) hiring
(B) to hire
(C) hired
(D) hire
Ⓐ Ⓑ Ⓒ Ⓓ

**17.** The CEO suggested that the new staff need -------- their communication skills through an intensive training course.
(A) developing
(B) to develop
(C) developed
(D) development
Ⓐ Ⓑ Ⓒ Ⓓ

**18.** After completing the questionnaire, the job candidates -------- in a group interview.
(A) participating
(B) to participate
(C) participated
(D) participation
Ⓐ Ⓑ Ⓒ Ⓓ

### Study Point Part 6 長文穴埋め問題

このパートでよく登場する文書の1つに手紙（letter）があります。TOEIC L&R TEST では、その手紙は友人に送るような個人的なものではなく、ビジネスに関連したものがほとんどです。そして、もちろん例外もありますが、以下のような順番で書かれていることが多いです。ぜひ知っておきましょう。

**1.** 簡単なあいさつ
例）Thank you for applying for the position of software engineer at JPIT.

**2.** 手紙を出した目的
例）We would like you to come to our office for an interview.

**3.** お願いしたいこと
例）Please let us know your schedule.

## Part 6 Text Completion

***Read a short text. Some words, phrases or sentences are missing from the text. Read the questions and choose the answer to complete the text.***

**Questions 19 to 22** refer to the following letter.

Kyle Robinson
2910 E. Harcourt Ave
Seattle, WA 96038

Dear Mr. Robinson,

We are happy to offer you the position of sales associate at McGilly Corp. Congratulations on this accomplishment. There were many qualified applicants, -------(**19.**) we felt your experience with software sales while at your previous company made you a unique fit for our needs. If you -------(**20.**) to accept this offer, please sign the enclosed contract in the three blanks -------(**21.**) with a red dot. -------(**22.**) .

Sincerely,

Jane Wilson
Personnel Director
McGilly Corp.

**19.** (A) as
(B) but
(C) for
(D) so
Ⓐ Ⓑ Ⓒ Ⓓ

**20.** (A) decide
(B) decision
(C) decides
(D) deciding
Ⓐ Ⓑ Ⓒ Ⓓ

**21.** (A) having marked
(B) marked
(C) marking
(D) will mark
Ⓐ Ⓑ Ⓒ Ⓓ

**22.** (A) After that is completed, we can decide the day for your interview.
(B) Be sure to sign it and date it and then mail it back to us soon.
(C) This document is only available by accessing our Web site.
(D) We are very glad to know that you have decided to join our company.
Ⓐ Ⓑ Ⓒ Ⓓ

**Study Point** Part 7 読解問題

Unit 3 で同義語を選ぶ問題について説明しました。今回はそれ以外の設問を紹介します。

1. 全体の内容を問う問題
   例) What is the article mainly about?
2. 個別の詳細な内容を問う問題
   例) Why did Mr. Thompson send the e-mail?
3. 書き手の意図を推測させる問題
   例) At 11:37 A.M., what does Ms. Wong mean when she writes, "He's pleased to do it"?
4. 文が入る適切な場所を問う問題
   * Unit 5 で詳しく説明します。

## Part 7  Single Passage

***Read the text and the questions following the text. Select the best answer for each question.***

**Questions 23 to 26** refer to the following letter.

Zamir Moore
Electrical and Computer Engineering Department
Electrovir Corporation
Sventon Building, Level 5

August 3

Dear Mr. Moore,

Thank you so much for offering me the opportunity to work at Electrovir Corporation as an electrical engineering assistant. As you may remember during our previous meeting, I mentioned that I was also applying to various universities that provide master's degree engineering programs. I received the news yesterday that I was accepted into my program of choice. Because of this, I am sorry to say that I will have to decline your generous offer at this time, as the program will start this coming fall. I know that it would be more beneficial for me to build my knowledge in graduate school first before working full-time in a company.

Once again, I would like to express my gratitude for your offer. I hope that we can continue to keep in touch, as I would definitely like to explore working in Electrovir Corporation when my studies are completed. Thank you again for your time.

Sincerely,

*Fiona Jannsen*
Fiona Jannsen

**23.** What is the purpose of the letter?
(A) To negotiate the terms of an employment contract
(B) To provide a summary of work experience
(C) To request more information about a company
(D) To turn down a job opportunity

Ⓐ Ⓑ Ⓒ Ⓓ

**24.** What is implied about Ms. Jannsen?
(A) She has completed a bachelor's degree.
(B) She will change her specialty.
(C) She intends to relocate in the near future.
(D) She is still seeking employment.

Ⓐ Ⓑ Ⓒ Ⓓ

**25.** What will Ms. Jannsen do in the fall?
(A) Begin an educational course
(B) Take time off for family reasons
(C) Start a new business
(D) Work in a company abroad

Ⓐ Ⓑ Ⓒ Ⓓ

**26.** Why does Ms. Jannsen want to remain in contact with Mr. Moore?
(A) To consider the possibility of employment in the future
(B) To introduce potential customers to him
(C) To partner with him on a business venture
(D) To request his advice about engineering

Ⓐ Ⓑ Ⓒ Ⓓ

## Review Exercise

***Read this shorter version of the letter in Part 7. Fill in appropriate words in the blank spaces from the box below.***

Thank you for [1]__________ me a job at Electrovir Corporation. I mentioned that, while job [2]__________, I have also been [3]__________ for master's degree programs. In fact, I have been accepted for such a program and must [4]__________ your kind offer. I am sorry to [5]__________ this news, but I do believe that further education will help me to develop my [6]__________. I hope that I may stay in [7]__________ with you, and I will certainly apply to Electrovir Corporation again for [8]__________, once my master's degree course is finished.

| | | | |
|---|---|---|---|
| (a) knowledge | (b) offering | (c) contact | (d) applying |
| (e) refuse | (f) hunting | (g) employment | (h) report |

MEMO

UNIT 05

# Entertainment and Leisure

## Vocabulary Exercise

*Match each English word with its meaning in Japanese.*

**1.** admission (　　)　**2.** equipment (　　)　**3.** box office (　　)　**4.** renewal (　　)
**5.** organizer (　　)　**6.** state-of-the-art (　　)　**7.** competition (　　)
**8.** applause (　　)　**9.** detailed (　　)　**10.** annual (　　)

a. 更新　b. 主催者　c. 競技会、競争　d. 入場（料）　e. 詳細な　f. 機器、備品
g. 最先端の、最新式の　h. 年１回の　i. 拍手喝采　j. チケット売り場

# LISTENING SECTION

## Dictation Exercise

*Listen to the following sentences. Fill in the blank spaces.*

1. Here is the weather forecast. Take care tomorrow as a typhoon is ______________ the coast.
2. I haven't seen Mr. Phelps in a ______________, so I'm looking forward to this week's meeting.
3. Please keep your ________________ to enter the prize draw after the movie.
4. During the ________________ call, the performers all bowed gracefully to the audience.
5. I need a quiet space with no ________________ in order to finish this report.

**Study Point**　Part 1　写真描写問題

写真に写る複数の人物の動作や状態が非常に似ているときは、そこに注意が向きがちですが、以下の問題のように、それ以外の部分の描写が正解になるケースもあります。

**A.** People are talking to each other.
**B.** People are watching a sports program.
**C.** Curtains are being opened.
**D.** A desk is unoccupied.

正解は D（机は誰にも使われていない）です。

## Part 1 ›› Photographs

1-51, 52

***Look at the picture and listen to four statements. Choose one statement that best describes the situation in the picture.***

1.

Ⓐ Ⓑ Ⓒ Ⓓ

2.

Ⓐ Ⓑ Ⓒ Ⓓ

### Study Point　Part 2 応答問題

Unit 3 のところで、肯定文の文末に **right?** を付けて「～ですよね?」と確認する問いかけについて説明しました。その場合には、**Yes** や **Correct** などから答えを始めることが多いですが、**right?** が付かない肯定文でも **Yes** から文を開始するケースがあります。以下の例を参照してください。

**Q1.** It's really windy out there.（外は本当に風が強いです）
**A1.** **Yes.** I nearly lost my hat.（そうですね。私はもう少しで帽子をなくすところでした）

**Q2.** That sure was a bumpy flight.（あれは本当にガタガタ揺れるフライトでした）
**A2.** **Yes**, but the pilot and crew were so calming.
（そうですね、でもパイロットとクルーはとても落ち着いていました）

## Part 2 Question-Response

*Listen to a question or statement and three responses. Choose the best response to the question or statement.*

3. Mark your answer on your answer sheet. Ⓐ Ⓑ Ⓒ
4. Mark your answer on your answer sheet. Ⓐ Ⓑ Ⓒ
5. Mark your answer on your answer sheet. Ⓐ Ⓑ Ⓒ
6. Mark your answer on your answer sheet. Ⓐ Ⓑ Ⓒ
7. Mark your answer on your answer sheet. Ⓐ Ⓑ Ⓒ

### Study Point Part 3 会話問題

このパートでは、会話中の人物が誰なのかや何の仕事をしているのかがよく聞かれます。複数の聞き方があるので紹介します。

1.「誰なのか（=職業は何なのか）」を聞く場合
Who is the man? / Who most likely is the woman?

2.「仕事は何か」を聞く場合
What is the man's **job**? ／ What most likely is the woman's **occupation**?
Where does the man probably **work**?（その男性はおそらくどこで働いていますか）
**In** what **field** does the woman most likely **work**?
（その女性はどの分野で働いていると考えられますか）

## Part 3 Conversation

*Listen to a conversation between two people. Read the questions on your answer sheet. Choose the best answer for each question.*

8. Who is the woman?
   (A) A box office clerk
   (B) A movie critic
   (C) An audience member
   (D) A screenwriter Ⓐ Ⓑ Ⓒ Ⓓ

9. What problem does the woman mention?
   (A) The cost of tickets is increasing.
   (B) The movie is too long.
   (C) Her children could not understand the movie.
   (D) The theater is overcrowded.
   Ⓐ Ⓑ Ⓒ Ⓓ

10. What does the man offer?
   (A) A gift certificate
   (B) A refund
   (C) Different seats
   (D) Free parking Ⓐ Ⓑ Ⓒ Ⓓ

## Study Point　Part 4　説明文問題

このパートではさまざま種類のアナウンスが流れます。ここではテーマパークの園内アナウンスを例にとって、基本的な流れをおさえます。

1. 挨拶
   例）We hope you're enjoying your day at the Magical Lake Theme Park.
   （マジカルレイク・テーマパークでの１日をお楽しみいただけていることを願っています）
2. 目的
   例）I'd like to tell you about a free movie ticket promotion that we're offering.
   （当テーマパークが提供中の映画チケット無料キャンペーンについてお知らせします）
3. 追加の情報（結び）
   例）After the movie has finished, the director will be giving a short talk.
   （映画終了後、監督の短いトークがあります）
   * 謝辞がないままトークが終わるケースも多々あるので、注意しましょう。

## Part 4 Talk

***Listen to a talk given by a single speaker. Read the questions on your answer sheet. Choose the best answer for each question.***

**11.** In what location is the announcement most likely taking place?
(A) A dance performance
(B) A music concert
(C) A play
(D) A sports competition
Ⓐ Ⓑ Ⓒ Ⓓ

**12.** What does the speaker ask the listeners to do?
(A) Hold their applause until later
(B) Stop talking
(C) Turn off their phones
(D) Visit the snack bar in the lobby
Ⓐ Ⓑ Ⓒ Ⓓ

**13.** What is available for purchase after the event?
(A) Beverages
(B) Photographs
(C) Mobile phones
(D) Videos
Ⓐ Ⓑ Ⓒ Ⓓ

# READING SECTION

## Study Point Part 5 短文穴埋め問題

### 受動態

※受動態の問題を解く際は、「主語が～する」なのか「主語が～される」なのか、よく考えましょう。

**〈by ＋動作主〉が省略される場合**

① 動作主が漠然とした人を指す
This concert hall **is** no longer **used** so often.
（このコンサートホールは、もはやそんなに頻繁には使用されていない）

② 動作主をあえて表す必要がない
Letters **are delivered** only once a day in this area.
（この地域では手紙は 1 日 1 回しか配達されない）

③ 動作主が誰かわからない
The old castle in Ireland **was built** around 1400.
（アイルランドにあるその古い城は 1400 年頃に建てられた）

**by 以外の前置詞を用いる受動態**

① The actor's name **is known** ***to*** everyone in the country.
（その俳優の名前はその国の皆に知られている）

② Small children **are** often **scared** ***of*** barking dogs.
（小さな子供たちは吠える犬をよく怖がる）

③ Some fans **were disappointed** ***with*** the band's performance.
（一部のファンはそのバンドの演奏にがっかりした）

☞以下の受動態も知っておきましょう。
**be covered *with*** ～（～に覆われている） **be tired *of*** ～（～にうんざりしている）
**be caught *in*** ～（～に巻き込まれる） **be related *to*** ～（～関連している）

**受動態にならない他動詞** （* 自動詞は目的語をとらないため受動態にはならない）

① Many people **lack** accurate information about available services.
（多くの人が利用可能なサービスに関する情報を持っていない）
*Accurate information about available services is lacked ... は不可です。

② A tour around the island **costs** 50 dollars per person.
（その島を巡るツアーは 1 人につき 50 ドルです）

③ This famous theater **holds** 9,000 people.（この有名な劇場は 9 千人収容できる）
*「開く」という意味の hold であれば以下のような受動態が作れます。
例）The meeting **was held** here.（その会議はここで開かれた）

☞以下の意味の他動詞も受動態を作れません。
**fit**（合う）/ **resemble**（似る）/ **possess**（所有する）/ **meet**（会う）

**間違えやすい例**

① This textbook **consists** (× is consisted) of 14 chapters in total.
（この教科書は全部で 14 章から成る）* A **is composed** of B. であれば可能です。

② The parade will **take place** (× be taken place) unless it rains.
（パレードは雨が降らない限り行われる）

## Part 5 Incomplete Sentences

***A word or phrase is missing in each of the sentences below. Choose the best word or phrase to complete the sentence.***

**14.** At the last minute, the organizer announced that the concert had been -------- due to stormy weather.
(A) cancel
(B) canceled
(C) canceling
(D) to cancel
Ⓐ Ⓑ Ⓒ Ⓓ

**15.** StarLight Stage Inc. will only -------- tickets for the performance to registered users of its Web site.
(A) to offer
(B) offering
(C) offer
(D) be offered
Ⓐ Ⓑ Ⓒ Ⓓ

**16.** At the award ceremony, the violinist Chloe Edwards -------- for her contribution to classical music.
(A) was honored
(B) honored
(C) honoring
(D) has honored
Ⓐ Ⓑ Ⓒ Ⓓ

**17.** The Wellington Planetarium is equipped -------- state-of-the-art technology that can project over a million stars.
(A) by
(B) in
(C) of
(D) with
Ⓐ Ⓑ Ⓒ Ⓓ

**18.** My section manager -------- a famous actor so he is often stopped by people in public places.
(A) resembles
(B) is resembled
(C) resembling
(D) to resemble
Ⓐ Ⓑ Ⓒ Ⓓ

### Study Point Part 6 長文穴埋め問題

イベントの告知や、新店舗オープンのお知らせには、多くの人たちの参加を促すための決まった表現がよく使われます。知っておくと便利です。

**1.** Join us for a complimentary investment seminar.
（無料の投資セミナーに参加してください）

**2.** Come visit the new Hanson Gallery in Vancouver.
（バンクーバーに新しくオープンしたハンソン・ギャラリーに来てください）

**3.** Feel free to take a guided tour of the Brantford campus.
（ブラントフォードキャンパスのガイドツアーにご自由にご参加ください）

**4.** I would like to invite you to our 10th anniversary celebration.
（私たちの 10 周年のお祝いにご招待いたします）

**5.** Please bring your family to enjoy a day at the Morton Museum.
（ご家族を連れてモートン・ミュージアムでの 1 日をお楽しみください）

## Part 6 Text Completion

***Read a short text. Some words, phrases or sentences are missing from the text. Read the questions and choose the answer to complete the text.***

**Questions 19 to 22** refer to the following information.

> The 32nd Annual Carsonville Community Fair will be the biggest and best yet! The program will include free live -------**19.** all day, more than 50 market stalls, and a wide variety of amusement for the children. There will be food trucks -------**20.** a wonderful array of food and drinks, hot meat pies, ice cream, and specialty coffees. Bring the whole family to the fair which -------**21.** on Sunday, June 20 from 10:00 A.M. to 4:00 P.M. at the Carsonville Fairgrounds on Highway 51. -------**22.** . Some of these include The Carsonville Moms Support Group, The Green Cross, and Science Equipment for Schools.

**19.** (A) entertain
(B) entertained
(C) entertaining
(D) entertainment
Ⓐ Ⓑ Ⓒ Ⓓ

**20.** (A) will sell
(B) are sold
(C) sell
(D) selling
Ⓐ Ⓑ Ⓒ Ⓓ

**21.** (A) had been held
(B) has been held
(C) is held
(D) will be held
Ⓐ Ⓑ Ⓒ Ⓓ

**22.** (A) Admission is just $25 for a family pass and $10 for individuals.
(B) All proceeds will go to local community groups and charities.
(C) For more detailed information, visit www.carsonvillefair.org/32.
(D) There is plenty of free car and bicycle parking at the fairgrounds.
Ⓐ Ⓑ Ⓒ Ⓓ

**Study Point** Part 7 読解問題

Unit 4で説明しきれなかった**文が入る適切な場所を問う問題**についてお伝えします。この設問は、指定された1文が本文中の4つの場所のどこに入るのが最も適当なのかを問うものです。他の設問よりも解答に時間がかかることがあるので、場合によっては後回しにしてもよいかもしれません。形式は以下の通りです。

In which of the positions marked [1], [2], [3], and [4] does the following sentence best belong?
"We truly appreciate your great effort."
(A) [1]
(B) [2]
(C) [3]
(D) [4]

## Part 7 Single Passage

***Read the text and the questions following the text. Select the best answer for each question.***

**Questions 23 to 26** refer to the following e-mail.

| | |
|---|---|
| To: | bcc <all customers> |
| From: | Olivia Maxwell <maxwell@watchcinema.com> |
| Date: | May 1 |
| Subject: | Get a 20% discount! |

Dear Customers,

Thank you for your subscription to WatchCinema.com, the Internet's biggest and best online movie streaming service. ---[1]---

---[2]--- I am pleased to announce that, for a limited time only, customers who change their automatic renewal service from monthly renewal to annual renewal will receive a 20% discount for a year's subscription. This special offer is only available this week. ---[3]---

To receive your discount, log in to our service as normal, click on "subscription settings" and then simply check the box "annual renewal." ---[4]---

We look forward to getting your subscription update.

Sincerely,
Olivia Maxwell
Subscriptions Manager

**23.** What is the purpose of the e-mail?
(A) To get new customers
(B) To warn about spam mail
(C) To announce a special offer
(D) To advertise a new Internet service
Ⓐ Ⓑ Ⓒ Ⓓ

**24.** What should customers do to obtain the discount?
(A) Renew their personal information
(B) Change the frequency of renewal
(C) Introduce a friend to the service
(D) Resister a credit card for automatic renewals
Ⓐ Ⓑ Ⓒ Ⓓ

**25.** In which of the positions marked [1], [2], [3], and [4] does the following sentence best belong?
"Act quickly to make sure you get your discount."
(A) [1]
(B) [2]
(C) [3]
(D) [4]
Ⓐ Ⓑ Ⓒ Ⓓ

**26.** According to the instructions, what is indicated about the process to receive the discount?
(A) It will be carried out automatically.
(B) It is not necessary to change the settings.
(C) A confirmation e-mail will be sent afterwards.
(D) Customers must access the service first.
Ⓐ Ⓑ Ⓒ Ⓓ

## Review Exercise

***Read this shorter version of the e-mail in Part 7. Fill in appropriate words in the blank spaces from the box below.***

Dear Customer,

[1]__________ for using WatchCinema.com, the [2]__________ online movie streaming service. [3]__________ your [4]__________ from monthly to annual and enjoy a 20% [5]__________ for one year. This [6]__________ is available only this week. To activate, [7]__________ , go to "subscription settings," and [8]__________ "annual renewal."

Sincerely,
Olivia Maxwell
Subscriptions Manager

| | | | |
|---|---|---|---|
| **(a)** switch | **(b)** log in | **(c)** subscription | **(d)** thank you |
| **(e)** offer | **(f)** largest | **(g)** select | **(h)** discount |

MEMO

UNIT 06

# Purchasing

## Vocabulary Exercise

*Match each English word with its meaning in Japanese.*

**1.** invoice (  ) **2.** warehouse (  ) **3.** defective (  ) **4.** package (  )
**5.** fragile (  ) **6.** grocery (  ) **7.** vendor (  ) **8.** shipment (  )
**9.** premises (  ) **10.** inspection (  )

a. 販売業者 b. 食料雑貨類 c. 倉庫 d. 検査 e. 壊れやすい
f. 欠陥のある g. 請求書 h. 小包、荷物 i. 積み荷 j. 敷地、構内

# LISTENING SECTION

## Dictation Exercise

*Listen to the following sentences. Fill in the blank spaces.*

1. SpeedPost is ________________ my order today, so I must be at home until it arrives.
2. Prices for our products including ________________ are indicated on our Web site.
3. Sarah is starting a new job next week, so these flowers are to wish her ________________.
4. The item was not packed in the box correctly and was ________________ damaged in transit.
5. The delivery company ________________ us a refund. We paid for next-day delivery, but the parcel arrived three days later.

**Study Point** Part 1 写真描写問題

写真の主役がものの場合、その状態を説明するために以下のような受動態がよく使用されます。知らない表現があれば、この機会に覚えましょう。

**1. be piled (up) / be stacked (up)** [ 積み上げられる ]
**2. be loaded** [ 積み込まれる ]
**3. be installed** [ 設置される ]
**4. be lined up** [ 並べられる ]
**5. be gathered** [ 集められる ]

## Part 1 Photographs

***Look at the picture and listen to four statements. Choose one statement that best describes the situation in the picture.***

1.

Ⓐ Ⓑ Ⓒ Ⓓ

2.

Ⓐ Ⓑ Ⓒ Ⓓ

### Study Point Part 2 応答問題

今回は疑問文の問いかけに対して疑問文で答える例をいくつか紹介します。

Q1: Should I buy this black sweater or the blue one?
(この黒いセーターを買うべきですか、それとも青い方を買うべきですか)
A1: **Which one is warmer?** (どちらの方が暖かいですか)

Q2: Why has the conference room been reserved all day?
(なぜその会議室は終日予約されているのですか)
A2: **Do you need it for a meeting?** (会議のためにその部屋が必要ですか)

Q3: Who's going to the post office today?
(今日は誰が郵便局に行くことになっていますか)
A3: **Do you have a package to send?** (送る小包があるのですか)

## Part 2 Question-Response

***Listen to a question or statement and three responses. Choose the best response to the question or statement.***

3. Mark your answer on your answer sheet. Ⓐ Ⓑ Ⓒ
4. Mark your answer on your answer sheet. Ⓐ Ⓑ Ⓒ
5. Mark your answer on your answer sheet. Ⓐ Ⓑ Ⓒ
6. Mark your answer on your answer sheet. Ⓐ Ⓑ Ⓒ
7. Mark your answer on your answer sheet. Ⓐ Ⓑ Ⓒ

**Study Point** Part 3 会話問題

このパートでは理由を尋ねる設問もよく出されます。その場合の答え方には、以下のように2パターンあります。

Q : Why is the woman at a computer store?
A1: She wants to buy a new PC.
A2: To buy a new PC
※特に **to 不定詞**で答えるタイプは、選択肢が短い場合が多いので、音声が流れる前に必ず内容を確認しておきましょう。

## Part 3 Conversation

***Listen to a conversation between two people. Read the questions on your answer sheet. Choose the best answer for each question.***

8. Why is the woman calling?
(A) To place an order
(B) To open a new business
(C) To change a delivery time
(D) To ask about popular flower types
Ⓐ Ⓑ Ⓒ Ⓓ

9. What does the man say about deliveries?
(A) They begin at midday.
(B) They are unavailable on Tuesdays.
(C) They include a complimentary gift.
(D) They are free of charge.
Ⓐ Ⓑ Ⓒ Ⓓ

10. What is the woman concerned about?
(A) How the flowers will be packaged
(B) How much the total cost will be
(C) How long the flowers will last
(D) How many flowers are available
Ⓐ Ⓑ Ⓒ Ⓓ

## Study Point Part 4 説明文問題

Unit 3 の Part 3 で、以下の例文を挙げて話し手の意図を問う問題について説明しました。

What does the man **mean** when he says, "**I helped Alex fix his webcam last week**"?

Part 4 でもこのタイプの問題はよく出されます。そして Part 3 でも Part 4 でも、以下のように聞き方が若干異なる場合があります。ですが、基本的に何か大きな違いが生じるわけではないので、冷静に対処しましょう。

What does the man **imply** when he says, "I've tried a lot of other applications like this"?

*__imply__ は「示唆する・暗示する」という意味の動詞です。

## Part 4 Talk

***Listen to a talk given by a single speaker. Read the questions on your answer sheet. Choose the best answer for each question.***

**11.** What problem does the speaker mention?
(A) A delivery company went out of business.
(B) An order got damaged.
(C) A product is defective.
(D) A shipment was sent to the wrong address. Ⓐ Ⓑ Ⓒ Ⓓ

**12.** What are the listeners asked to do?
(A) Choose a delivery company
(B) Put items in boxes
(C) Send shipments to a different address
(D) Contact the warehouse staff Ⓐ Ⓑ Ⓒ Ⓓ

**13.** What does the speaker imply when he says, "Then I will be busy dealing with the original delivery company"?
(A) He will not have time to pack any boxes today.
(B) He will negotiate a refund with a company.
(C) He wants the delivery company to give him a discount.
(D) He wants the workers to help him with deliveries. Ⓐ Ⓑ Ⓒ Ⓓ

# READING SECTION

**Study Point** Part 5 短文穴埋め問題

## 接続詞

**while ①「時」～する間に ②「対比」（ところで）一方**

① The delivery man was stuck in traffic **while** (he was) delivering the package.
（その配達員は荷物を運んでいる間に渋滞に巻き込まれた）
*while の後には進行形や状態動詞（例 while they're on vacation）がよく続きます。

② She is in Mexico, **while** her brother is in Turkey.
（彼女はメキシコにいるが、一方、彼女の弟はトルコにいる）
*while の前後の文の関係性に着目しましょう。

**since ①「時」～して以来 ②「原因・理由」～なので**

① I haven't seen the teacher **since** I graduated from junior high school.
（中学校を卒業して以来、その先生には会っていない）
* 主節の動詞は**現在完了形**か**過去完了形**で、since の後ろは**過去形**になることが多いです。またこのような場合、since は通常後ろに来ます。

② **Since** he is so busy, he doesn't have time to eat lunch.
（彼はとても忙しいので、昼食を食べる時間がない）
* この場合は文頭に来ることが多いです。また、同じ意味の As も使われます。

**so ① so ~ that ...「非常に～なので…（結果）」 ② so that「～するために（目的）」**

① The box was **so** heavy **(that)** I couldn't lift it at all. *that は省略可です。
（その箱はとても重かったので、持ち上げることがまったくできなかった）

② The meeting time was changed **so (that)** the CEO could attend.
（CEO が参加できるように会議の時間が変更された）*that は省略可です。
*can や could などの助動詞を伴うことが多いですが、助動詞がないこともあります。
例）New patients should come early **so (that)** they *have* time to complete the required paperwork.
（新患の人は必要書類の作成時間を確保するために早めに来院した方がよい）

**unless 「～しない限り」**

The park will remain open **unless** it rains hard.
（その公園は雨が激しく降らない限り開園している）
*unless には否定の意味が含まれているので、後ろの節の中で not は使用しません。

**once 「ひとたび～すれば」**

**Once** the order has been placed, you can't change the delivery address.
= If the order has been placed **once**, you can't change the delivery address.
（ひとたび注文が完了すると、届け先の住所を変更することはできない）
* 前者の Once は接続詞ですが、後者の once は副詞です。

## Part 5 Incomplete Sentences

***A word or phrase is missing in each of the sentences below. Choose the best word or phrase to complete the sentence.***

**14.** The delivery arrived -------- Ms. Sousa was out of the office, so I signed for it on her behalf and left it on her desk.
(A) while
(B) so
(C) since
(D) unless
Ⓐ Ⓑ Ⓒ Ⓓ

**15.** PackagePower's delivery service has been -------- good that we have been using them exclusively.
(A) to
(B) over
(C) so
(D) more
Ⓐ Ⓑ Ⓒ Ⓓ

**16.** Customers get an e-mail notification just before delivery and a confirmation -------- the delivery has been completed.
(A) unless
(B) by
(C) once
(D) while
Ⓐ Ⓑ Ⓒ Ⓓ

**17.** Groman Industries Inc. placed an order for three electric generators -------- specified delivery to their Atlanta facility.
(A) or
(B) and
(C) instead
(D) because
Ⓐ Ⓑ Ⓒ Ⓓ

**18.** The delivery of the new security equipment will be a day late -------- it is undergoing a customs inspection at the airport.
(A) but
(B) yet
(C) thus
(D) as
Ⓐ Ⓑ Ⓒ Ⓓ

### Study Point Part 6 長文穴埋め問題

TOEIC L&R TEST では、最後の Part 7 **にいかに多くの時間を残せるか**が勝負のカギになります。そのため、このパートでは短い時間で効率よく解答することが重要です。ここでの出題パターンは**語彙・文法問題**と**空所に入る 1 文を選択する問題**の 2 つです。問題を上から順に解きたいと思う人もいるかもしれませんが、**文の選択問題**の方が難易度が高いので、**語彙・文法問題**から解いていきましょう。

[ Question 20-21 ]
I have ordered supplies from you for several years and have never experienced a delay like this. -------- (20.). If I do not get a ------- (21.) response from you within 24 hours, I will have to ...
* 語彙問題の Q21 から先に解きましょう。

## Part 6 Text Completion

***Read a short text. Some words, phrases or sentences are missing from the text. Read the questions and choose the answer to complete the text.***

**Questions 19 to 22** refer to the following e-mail.

To: Office Outfitters <cs@outfitters.net>
From: Jessica Bradley <jbradley@jbtesq.net>
Date: July 5
Subject: My order

Dear Customer Service,

I ordered 11 boxes of copy paper from you last Monday and have ------- **19.** to receive them. I have ordered supplies from you for several years and have never experienced a delay like this. ------- **20.** . If I do not get a ------- **21.** response from you within 24 hours, I will have to cancel my order and take my business to one of your competitors.

Thank you for your prompt ------- **22.** to this matter.

Sincerely,

Jessica Bradley

Johnson, Bell, and Thomas, Esq.

**19.** (A) already
(B) never
(C) still
(D) yet

Ⓐ Ⓑ Ⓒ Ⓓ

**20.** (A) As far as I know, we have paid our invoices on time for the past three months.
(B) I'm afraid I cannot wait any longer and will be searching for a different vendor.
(C) Please let me know what happened to my order and when I can expect delivery.
(D) When the order arrives, I will divide the copy paper among the four departments.

Ⓐ Ⓑ Ⓒ Ⓓ

**21.** (A) satisfaction
(B) satisfactorily
(C) satisfactory
(D) satisfy

Ⓐ Ⓑ Ⓒ Ⓓ

**22.** (A) attend
(B) attending
(C) attends
(D) attention

Ⓐ Ⓑ Ⓒ Ⓓ

**Study Point** Part 7 読解問題

このパートでは1つの文書だけでなく、2つの文書、または3つの文書を扱う問題も出されます。内訳は以下の通りです。問題数を意識して時間内に解答していきましょう。

| | | |
|---|---|---|
| シングルパッセージ問題 | **1つの文書**を読んで**2～4問**の設問に答える | 合計**10題** |
| ダブルパッセージ問題 | **2つの文書**を読んで**5問**の設問に答える | 合計**2題** |
| トリプルパッセージ問題 | **3つの文書**を読んで**5問**の設問に答える | 合計**3題** |

* 例えば、以下の文言で文書の数が判断できます。
Questions 23 to 26 refer to the following **e-mail.** → シングルパッセージ問題
Questions 23 to 27 refer to the following **e-mail and table.** → ダブルパッセージ問題
Questions 23 to 27 refer to the following **e-mails and table.** → トリプルパッセージ問題

## Part 7 Double Passages

***Read the text and the questions following the text. Select the best answer for each question.***

**Questions 23 to 27** refer to the following e-mail and table.

To: Sophia Lambert <lamberts@kru-tech.com>
From: Michael O'Connor <oconnor@dartdelivery.com>
Date: April 15
Subject: Delivery to Atlanta

Dear Ms. Lambert,

Thank you very much for contacting Dart Delivery Services. In regard to your inquiry, I have attached a list of our most popular delivery options. You have indicated that the total weight of the items that you want delivered to Atlanta will be exactly 9.8 kilograms, without any packaging materials. Please be aware that, as these are ceramic items, packaging is essential and this will increase the weight by at least 300 grams. Your requirement of next-day delivery is certainly possible, although as you can see from the table this will increase the cost considerably. For that reason, I would recommend a slightly longer delivery time, if that is acceptable to your customer.

Please let me know your final decision by return mail and then I will arrange for a pickup at your company premises this afternoon.

Best regards,

Michael O'Connor

Delivery Manager

| Delivery Plan | Maximum weight (Kg) | Maximum Size (L+W+H,cm) | Delivery Time to Atlanta | Cost | Insurance |
|---|---|---|---|---|---|
| Economy | 5 | 100 | 5 days | $75 | Not available |
| Standard | 10 | 200 | 3 days | $100 | Available as an option |
| Premium | 20 | 400 | 48 hours | $200 | Included (up to $5000) |
| Elite | 50 | 600 | Next day | $600 | Included (unlimited) |

**23.** What does Mr. O'Connor indicate in his e-mail?
(A) Ms. Lambert is a regular customer of Dart Delivery Services.
(B) He is replying to an e-mail from Ms. Lambert.
(C) His e-mail to Ms. Lambert is late.
(D) The problem will be dealt with today. Ⓐ Ⓑ Ⓒ Ⓓ

**24.** In the e-mail, the word "essential" in paragraph 1, line 5, is closest in meaning to
(A) available
(B) included
(C) effective
(D) necessary Ⓐ Ⓑ Ⓒ Ⓓ

**25.** What is suggested about the items?
(A) They are mass-produced.
(B) They are flexible.
(C) They are fragile.
(D) They are defective. Ⓐ Ⓑ Ⓒ Ⓓ

**26.** Which delivery plan does Mr. O'Connor likely recommend?
(A) Economy
(B) Standard
(C) Premium
(D) Elite Ⓐ Ⓑ Ⓒ Ⓓ

**27.** According to the table, what is indicated about insurance for Standard delivery?
(A) It is unavailable.
(B) It costs extra.
(C) It is a requirement.
(D) It is included in the cost.
Ⓐ Ⓑ Ⓒ Ⓓ

## Review Exercise

***Read this shorter version of the e-mail in Part 7. Fill in appropriate words in the blank spaces from the box below.***

Thank you for [1]__________ out to Dart Delivery Services. I've attached our popular delivery [2]__________ for your convenience. Your items' total [3]__________ is 9.8 kilograms without packaging. Considering they are ceramic items, packaging will [4]__________ around 300 grams to the weight. Next-day delivery is [5]__________ but pricey. I [6]__________ considering a slightly longer delivery time for a more budget-friendly option. Please confirm your [7]__________ via e-mail, and I will [8]__________ for pickup this afternoon at your company premises.

| | | | |
|---|---|---|---|
| **(a)** options | **(b)** suggest | **(c)** possible | **(d)** weight |
| **(e)** reaching | **(f)** arrange | **(g)** decision | **(h)** add |

MEMO

UNIT 07

# Review Unit 1

## LISTENING SECTION

### Part 1 Photographs

1-74

***Look at the picture and listen to four statements. Choose one statement that best describes the situation in the picture.***

1.

Ⓐ Ⓑ Ⓒ Ⓓ

2.

Ⓐ Ⓑ Ⓒ Ⓓ

## Part 2 Question-Response

1-75

***Listen to a question or statement and three responses. Choose the best response to the question or statement.***

3. Mark your answer on your answer sheet. Ⓐ Ⓑ Ⓒ

4. Mark your answer on your answer sheet. Ⓐ Ⓑ Ⓒ

5. Mark your answer on your answer sheet. Ⓐ Ⓑ Ⓒ

6. Mark your answer on your answer sheet. Ⓐ Ⓑ Ⓒ

7. Mark your answer on your answer sheet. Ⓐ Ⓑ Ⓒ

8. Mark your answer on your answer sheet. Ⓐ Ⓑ Ⓒ

## Part 3 Conversation

1-76

***Listen to a conversation between two people. Read the questions on your answer sheet. Choose the best answer for each question.***

9. According to the woman, what has changed about the project meeting?
(A) The number of participants
(B) The date
(C) The start time
(D) The meeting agenda
Ⓐ Ⓑ Ⓒ Ⓓ

10. Look at the graphic. Which room will probably be used?
(A) Room 102
(B) Room 107
(C) Room 203
(D) Room 301
Ⓐ Ⓑ Ⓒ Ⓓ

11. What does the man ask the woman to do?
(A) Order some refreshments
(B) Share new information
(C) Cancel a meeting
(D) Conduct a training workshop
Ⓐ Ⓑ Ⓒ Ⓓ

| Meeting Room | Capacity |
|---|---|
| Room 102 | Up to 6 people |
| Room 107 | Up to 24 people |
| Room 203 | Up to 12 people |
| Room 301 | Up to 4 people |

**12.** Why is the woman calling?
(A) To change an appointment
(B) To request more information
(C) To inquire about food items
(D) To make a reservation
Ⓐ Ⓑ Ⓒ Ⓓ

**13.** What is the woman concerned about?
(A) The cost of soy products
(B) Her husband's food allergy
(C) How she can access the location
(D) The opening and closing times
Ⓐ Ⓑ Ⓒ Ⓓ

**14.** What does the man mean when he says, "please be sure to remind your server when you order"?
(A) He hopes the woman does not forget her order.
(B) He suggests the woman tell the server about the special request.
(C) He thinks the woman might forget who her server is.
(D) He wants the woman to remember to tip the server.
Ⓐ Ⓑ Ⓒ Ⓓ

## Part 4 Talk

***Listen to a talk given by a single speaker. Read the questions on your answer sheet. Choose the best answer for each question.***

**15.** Who most likely is the speaker?
(A) An aircraft mechanic
(B) A travel agent
(C) A flight attendant
(D) An airline pilot
Ⓐ Ⓑ Ⓒ Ⓓ

**16.** What is the reason for the announcement?
(A) Bad weather
(B) Crew shortage
(C) Airplanes ahead
(D) Mechanical problems
Ⓐ Ⓑ Ⓒ Ⓓ

**17.** What does the speaker ask the listeners to do?
(A) Ask for a refund
(B) Call their family members
(C) Put away their laptops
(D) Remain seated
Ⓐ Ⓑ Ⓒ Ⓓ

**18.** Where does the speaker most likely work?

(A) Research and Development
(B) Human Resources
(C) Marketing
(D) Sales

Ⓐ Ⓑ Ⓒ Ⓓ

**19.** What does the speaker ask the listener to do?

(A) Ask his supervisor for some information
(B) Conduct interviews for job candidates
(C) Give a new employee orientation talk
(D) Ask his worker to submit a form

Ⓐ Ⓑ Ⓒ Ⓓ

**20.** What does the speaker want to do by the end of the workday?

(A) Complete a bank procedure
(B) Finish a report
(C) Interview candidates
(D) Meet with a coworker

Ⓐ Ⓑ Ⓒ Ⓓ

# READING SECTION

## Part 5  Incomplete Sentences

***A word or phrase is missing in each of the sentences below. Choose the best word or phrase to complete the sentence.***

**21.** In order to accommodate increased numbers of passengers, the airport authority -------- a new terminal building in the next financial year.
(A) to construct
(B) has constructed
(C) constructed
(D) is constructing
Ⓐ Ⓑ Ⓒ Ⓓ

**22.** Although Ms. Prasad had a long and -------- journey, she was on time for the meeting.
(A) tire
(B) tiring
(C) tired
(D) tires
Ⓐ Ⓑ Ⓒ Ⓓ

**23.** For this set course, there are only two options for the side dish, but -------- of the two will definitely be goood.
(A) those
(B) either
(C) also
(D) together
Ⓐ Ⓑ Ⓒ Ⓓ

**24.** Although HayTech Media was expected -------- eight new recruits, only five candidates submitted their applications.
(A) hiring
(B) to hire
(C) hired
(D) hire
Ⓐ Ⓑ Ⓒ Ⓓ

**25.** The Wellington Planetarium is equipped -------- state-of-the-art technology that can project over a million stars.
(A) by
(B) in
(C) of
(D) with
Ⓐ Ⓑ Ⓒ Ⓓ

**26.** The delivery arrived -------- Ms. Sousa was out of the office, so I signed for it on her behalf and left it on her desk.
(A) while
(B) so
(C) since
(D) unless
Ⓐ Ⓑ Ⓒ Ⓓ

## Part 6 Text Completion

***Read a short text. Some words, phrases or sentences are missing from the text. Read the questions and choose the answer to complete the text.***

**Questions 27 to 30** refer to the following information.

The 32nd Annual Carsonville Community Fair will be the biggest and best yet! The program will include free live ------- (**27.**) all day, more than 50 market stalls, and a wide variety of amusement for the children. There will be food trucks ------- (**28.**) a wonderful array of food and drinks, hot meat pies, ice cream, and specialty coffees. Bring the whole family to the fair which ------- (**29.**) on Sunday, June 20 from 10:00 A.M. to 4:00 P.M. at the Carsonville Fairgrounds on Highway 51. ------- (**30.**) . Some of these include The Carsonville Moms Support Group, The Green Cross, and Science Equipment for Schools.

**27.** (A) entertain
(B) entertained
(C) entertaining
(D) entertainment
Ⓐ Ⓑ Ⓒ Ⓓ

**28.** (A) will sell
(B) are sold
(C) sell
(D) selling
Ⓐ Ⓑ Ⓒ Ⓓ

**29.** (A) had been held
(B) has been held
(C) is held
(D) will be held
Ⓐ Ⓑ Ⓒ Ⓓ

**30.** (A) Admission is just $25 for a family pass and $10 for individuals.
(B) All proceeds will go to local community groups and charities.
(C) For more detailed information, visit www.carsonvillefair.org/32.
(D) There is plenty of free car and bicycle parking at the fairgrounds.
Ⓐ Ⓑ Ⓒ Ⓓ

**Questions 31 to 34** refer to the following e-mail.

To: Office Outfitters <cs@outfitters.net>
From: Jessica Bradley <jbradley@jbtesq.net>
Date: July 5
Subject: My order

Dear Customer Service,

I ordered 11 boxes of copy paper from you last Monday and have ------- **31.** to receive them. I have ordered supplies from you for several years and have never experienced a delay like this. ------- **32.** . If I do not get a ------- **33.** response from you within 24 hours, I will have to cancel my order and take my business to one of your competitors.

Thank you for your prompt ------- **34.** to this matter.

Sincerely,

Jessica Bradley

Johnson, Bell, and Thomas, Esq.

**31.** (A) already
(B) never
(C) still
(D) yet
Ⓐ Ⓑ Ⓒ Ⓓ

**32.** (A) As far as I know, we have paid our invoices on time for the past three months.
(B) I'm afraid I cannot wait any longer and will be searching for a different vendor.
(C) Please let me know what happened to my order and when I can expect delivery.
(D) When the order arrives, I will divide the copy paper among the four departments.
Ⓐ Ⓑ Ⓒ Ⓓ

**33.** (A) satisfaction
(B) satisfactorily
(C) satisfactory
(D) satisfy
Ⓐ Ⓑ Ⓒ Ⓓ

**34.** (A) attend
(B) attending
(C) attends
(D) attention
Ⓐ Ⓑ Ⓒ Ⓓ

## Part 7 Single Passage

***Read the text and the questions following the text. Select the best answer for each question.***

Questions 35 to 38 refer to the following online discussion.

**Andy Marquez (9:04 A.M.)**
Is everybody ready for the meeting? Remember, this one is important. If we can persuade TechStar to purchase our new products, we could get a lot of new business from other companies, too.

**Susan Littleton (9:06 A.M.)**
I think we're all good. I've got the new samples packed safely in a small case. Mark, how about the presentation?

**Mark Adeoye (9:09 A.M.)**
The slideshow is all done. I updated the pricing information based on Andy's e-mail of the day before yesterday, although I haven't indicated any information about possible discounts.

**Andy Marquez (9:12 A.M.)**
No, that's fine. It's too early to make any promises yet, but during the meeting I can give a general indication of the kind of discounts we can offer.

**Mark Adeoye (9:14 A.M.)**
By the way, how long do you think this will last? I need to be back in the office by 3:00.

**Andy Marquez (9:15 A.M.)**
Well, the meeting is scheduled for 11:00 to 1:00. Susan, what do you think? You're driving us there and back.

**Susan Littleton (9:17 A.M.)**
I've visited companies in the Hampton Industrial Park before. It only takes about 30 minutes to get there, even if the traffic is heavy. You'll be fine Mark.

**Mark Adeoye (9:18 A.M.)**
Thanks. Glad to know that.

**Andy Marquez (9:20 A.M.)**
Great. Anyway, I will see you both down in the lobby in about 20 minutes. An early start will give us time to grab a coffee and bagel on the way.

**35.** Who most likely are the writers?
(A) Accounts staff
(B) Sales staff
(C) Purchasing staff
(D) Human Resources staff

Ⓐ Ⓑ Ⓒ Ⓓ

**36.** At 9:06 A.M., what does Ms. Littleton mean when she writes, "I think we're all good"?
(A) The preparations are complete.
(B) All the new products are excellent.
(C) New business would be welcome.
(D) Other companies are acceptable, too.

Ⓐ Ⓑ Ⓒ Ⓓ

**37.** What is indicated about Mr. Marquez?
(A) He packed the samples himself.
(B) He will leave the discounting decisions to Mr. Adeoye.
(C) He cannot promise that he will attend the meeting.
(D) He contacted Mr. Adeoye earlier this week.

Ⓐ Ⓑ Ⓒ Ⓓ

**38.** Why does Mr. Marquez want to make an early start?
(A) To discuss the meeting agenda
(B) To avoid heavy traffic on the way
(C) To get some refreshments
(D) To hold a meeting in the lobby

Ⓐ Ⓑ Ⓒ Ⓓ

**Questions 39 to 42** refer to the following letter.

Zamir Moore
Electrical and Computer Engineering Department
Electrovir Corporation
Sventon Building, Level 5

August 3

Dear Mr. Moore,

Thank you so much for offering me the opportunity to work at Electrovir Corporation as an electrical engineering assistant. As you may remember during our previous meeting, I mentioned that I was also applying to various universities that provide master's degree engineering programs. I received the news yesterday that I was accepted into my program of choice. Because of this, I am sorry to say that I will have to decline your generous offer at this time, as the program will start this coming fall. I know that it would be more beneficial for me to build my knowledge in graduate school first before working full-time in a company.

Once again, I would like to express my gratitude for your offer. I hope that we can continue to keep in touch, as I would definitely like to explore working in Electrovir Corporation when my studies are completed. Thank you again for your time.

Sincerely,

*Fiona Jannsen*
Fiona Jannsen

**39.** What is the purpose of the letter?
(A) To negotiate the terms of an employment contract
(B) To provide a summary of work experience
(C) To request more information about a company
(D) To turn down a job opportunity
Ⓐ Ⓑ Ⓒ Ⓓ

**40.** What is implied about Ms. Jannsen?
(A) She has completed a bachelor's degree.
(B) She will change her specialty.
(C) She intends to relocate in the near future.
(D) She is still seeking employment.
Ⓐ Ⓑ Ⓒ Ⓓ

**41.** What will Ms. Jannsen do in the fall?
(A) Begin an educational course
(B) Take time off for family reasons
(C) Start a new business
(D) Work in a company abroad
Ⓐ Ⓑ Ⓒ Ⓓ

**42.** Why does Ms. Jannsen want to remain in contact with Mr. Moore?
(A) To consider the possibility of employment in the future
(B) To introduce potential customers to him
(C) To partner with him on a business venture
(D) To request his advice about engineering
Ⓐ Ⓑ Ⓒ Ⓓ

# Review Unit 1

学籍番号 ____________

名前 ____________

スコア　　　/42

| Listening Section | | | | |
|---|---|---|---|---|
| **Part 1** | | | | |
| No.1 | Ⓐ | Ⓑ | Ⓒ | Ⓓ |
| No.2 | Ⓐ | Ⓑ | Ⓒ | Ⓓ |
| **Part 2** | | | | |
| No.3 | Ⓐ | Ⓑ | Ⓒ | |
| No.4 | Ⓐ | Ⓑ | Ⓒ | |
| No.5 | Ⓐ | Ⓑ | Ⓒ | |
| No.6 | Ⓐ | Ⓑ | Ⓒ | |
| No.7 | Ⓐ | Ⓑ | Ⓒ | |
| No.8 | Ⓐ | Ⓑ | Ⓒ | |
| **Part 3** | | | | |
| No.9 | Ⓐ | Ⓑ | Ⓒ | Ⓓ |
| No.10 | Ⓐ | Ⓑ | Ⓒ | Ⓓ |
| No.11 | Ⓐ | Ⓑ | Ⓒ | Ⓓ |
| No.12 | Ⓐ | Ⓑ | Ⓒ | Ⓓ |
| No.13 | Ⓐ | Ⓑ | Ⓒ | Ⓓ |
| No.14 | Ⓐ | Ⓑ | Ⓒ | Ⓓ |
| **Part 4** | | | | |
| No.15 | Ⓐ | Ⓑ | Ⓒ | Ⓓ |
| No.16 | Ⓐ | Ⓑ | Ⓒ | Ⓓ |
| No.17 | Ⓐ | Ⓑ | Ⓒ | Ⓓ |
| No.18 | Ⓐ | Ⓑ | Ⓒ | Ⓓ |
| No.19 | Ⓐ | Ⓑ | Ⓒ | Ⓓ |
| No.20 | Ⓐ | Ⓑ | Ⓒ | Ⓓ |

| Reading Section | | | | |
|---|---|---|---|---|
| **Part 5** | | | | |
| No.21 | Ⓐ | Ⓑ | Ⓒ | Ⓓ |
| No.22 | Ⓐ | Ⓑ | Ⓒ | Ⓓ |
| No.23 | Ⓐ | Ⓑ | Ⓒ | Ⓓ |
| No.24 | Ⓐ | Ⓑ | Ⓒ | Ⓓ |
| No.25 | Ⓐ | Ⓑ | Ⓒ | Ⓓ |
| No.26 | Ⓐ | Ⓑ | Ⓒ | Ⓓ |
| **Part 6** | | | | |
| No.27 | Ⓐ | Ⓑ | Ⓒ | Ⓓ |
| No.28 | Ⓐ | Ⓑ | Ⓒ | Ⓓ |
| No.29 | Ⓐ | Ⓑ | Ⓒ | Ⓓ |
| No.30 | Ⓐ | Ⓑ | Ⓒ | Ⓓ |
| No.31 | Ⓐ | Ⓑ | Ⓒ | Ⓓ |
| No.32 | Ⓐ | Ⓑ | Ⓒ | Ⓓ |
| No.33 | Ⓐ | Ⓑ | Ⓒ | Ⓓ |
| No.34 | Ⓐ | Ⓑ | Ⓒ | Ⓓ |
| **Part 7** | | | | |
| No.35 | Ⓐ | Ⓑ | Ⓒ | Ⓓ |
| No.36 | Ⓐ | Ⓑ | Ⓒ | Ⓓ |
| No.37 | Ⓐ | Ⓑ | Ⓒ | Ⓓ |
| No.38 | Ⓐ | Ⓑ | Ⓒ | Ⓓ |
| No.39 | Ⓐ | Ⓑ | Ⓒ | Ⓓ |
| No.40 | Ⓐ | Ⓑ | Ⓒ | Ⓓ |
| No.41 | Ⓐ | Ⓑ | Ⓒ | Ⓓ |
| No.42 | Ⓐ | Ⓑ | Ⓒ | Ⓓ |

UNIT 08

# Health

## Vocabulary Exercise

***Match each English word with its meaning in Japanese.***

**1.** prescription (　　) **2.** install (　　) **3.** undergo (　　) **4.** publicize (　　)
**5.** furthermore (　　) **6.** fill in (= fill out) (　　) **7.** compensation (　　)
**8.** prolonged (　　) **9.** durable (　　) **10.** pharmacy (　　)

a. 取り付ける、設置する　b. さらに　c. 補償　d. 丈夫な　e. 宣伝する
f. 薬局　g. 処方薬（箋）　h. （検査などを）受ける　i. 長期の
j. 必要事項を記入する

# LISTENING SECTION

## Dictation Exercise

***Listen to the following sentences. Fill in the blank spaces.***

1. This ______________ leads to the locker room.
2. I got the results of my ______________ health checkup today and fortunately there were no problems.
3. Anthony was on sick leave last week, so the other members of staff ______________ his shifts.
4. Our regular business ______________ are 10:00 A.M. to 6:00 P.M.
5. Visitors can meet ______________ between 10:00 A.M. and 11:00 A.M.

**Study Point** Part 1　写真描写問題

複数の人物が写っている問題で、選択肢の主語がすべて異なる場合があります。さらに、ものが主語になることもあるので、まずは各選択肢の冒頭の音に集中しましょう。

**A.** The doctor is reaching out to a patient.
**B.** One of the men is lying on his back.
**C.** The woman is taking some notes.
**D.** Posters are being attached to the wall.

正解は C です。

## Part 1 Photographs

1-79, 80

***Look at the picture and listen to four statements. Choose one statement that best describes the situation in the picture.***

1.

Ⓐ Ⓑ Ⓒ Ⓓ

2.

Ⓐ Ⓑ Ⓒ Ⓓ

### Study Point Part 2 応答問題

〈前置詞+疑問詞〉の疑問文は、話し言葉だと堅い表現になってしまうので、特に、リスニングセクションでは以下のように、前置詞は文末に移動されます。是非、慣れておきましょう。

**For** what are you looking? → What are you looking **for**?

その他の例

Which aisle are the stationary products **in**?（文房具はどの通路にありますか）
What's today's presentation **about**?（今日のプレゼンは何についてですか）
Which conference are you going **to**?（あなたはどの会議に出ますか）

## Part 2 Question-Response

CD 1-81～85

***Listen to a question or statement and three responses. Choose the best response to the question or statement.***

3. Mark your answer on your answer sheet. Ⓐ Ⓑ Ⓒ
4. Mark your answer on your answer sheet. Ⓐ Ⓑ Ⓒ
5. Mark your answer on your answer sheet. Ⓐ Ⓑ Ⓒ
6. Mark your answer on your answer sheet. Ⓐ Ⓑ Ⓒ
7. Mark your answer on your answer sheet. Ⓐ Ⓑ Ⓒ

### Study Point Part 3 会話問題

**How much** や **How many, How long** などから始まる設問は、選択肢がシンプルなので正解しやすいように思うかもしれませんが、会話内容に以下のようなひねりが加えられているケースもあります。よく音声を聞いて解答しましょう。

例) How much will the woman receive as a discount?
"Everything in the shop is 30 percent off the price tag." → **店内全品 30% オフ**
"If you bring the coupon, it will give you an additional 20 percent off."
→ **クーポンを持参すれば、さらに 20% オフ**

## Part 3 Conversation

CD 1-86, 87

***Listen to a conversation between two people. Read the questions on your answer sheet. Choose the best answer for each question.***

8. Why is the woman calling?
   (A) To ask about a coworker's condition
   (B) To get approval on a budget item
   (C) To make a doctor's appointment
   (D) To remind a coworker of a deadline
   Ⓐ Ⓑ Ⓒ Ⓓ

9. How long will the man be absent from work?
   (A) A few days
   (B) A week
   (C) Two weeks
   (D) Three weeks
   Ⓐ Ⓑ Ⓒ Ⓓ

10. What does the woman ask the man to do?
    (A) Find a replacement worker
    (B) Give some information
    (C) See a different doctor
    (D) Come to the office
    Ⓐ Ⓑ Ⓒ Ⓓ

**Study Point** Part 4 説明文問題

前にも紹介したように、このパートでもトークに入る前に、そのトークの種類に応じて “Questions 11 through 13 refer to the following **advertisement**.” という指示文が流れます。この下線部の文言は、音声が流れる前にトーク全体をイメージする上で重要な役割を果たします。次の 2 種類のトークは特に混同しやすいので、注意が必要です

1. “Questions 11 through 13 refer to the following **recorded message**.”
   → 流れるのは**録音された自動応答メッセージ**です。
2. “Questions 11 through 13 refer to the following **telephone message**.”
   → 流れるのは**留守番電話に残されたメッセージ**です。

## Part 4 Talk

***Listen to a talk given by a single speaker. Read the questions on your answer sheet. Choose the best answer for each question.***

**11.** Who are the listeners?
(A) Medical staff
(B) Web site managers
(C) Receptionists
(D) Patients
Ⓐ Ⓑ Ⓒ Ⓓ

**12.** What does the speaker say about business hours?
(A) The clinic opens at 9:30 A.M.
(B) The clinic closes at 6:00 P.M.
(C) The clinic is open on weekdays.
(D) The clinic is closed every Friday.
Ⓐ Ⓑ Ⓒ Ⓓ

**13.** What will happen when Dr. Thomas is on vacation?
(A) The clinic will be closed.
(B) Patients should leave a telephone message.
(C) Another doctor will be available.
(D) Dr. Thomas will see patients online.
Ⓐ Ⓑ Ⓒ Ⓓ

# READING SECTION

## Study Point Part 5 短文穴埋め問題

### 形容詞／副詞

**形容詞**

A. 名詞を修飾する形容詞は**形容詞＋名詞**が原則だが、次の場合は**名詞＋形容詞**になる

1. -thing, -body, -one で終わる不定代名詞を修飾する場合
   He was taken to the hospital, but doctors could not find anything **wrong**.
   （彼は病院に運ばれたが、医師たちは異常を見つけることができなかった）
2. -able, -ible で終わる形容詞が最上級や all, any, every などを強める場合
   This is one of the best fitness gyms **available** around here.
   （ここはこの辺りで利用できる最高のフィットネスジムのひとつだ）
   *an available fitness gym（利用可能なフィットネスジム）と言うこともできます。
3. 形容詞に他の語句が付いて 2 語以上の語群を形成する場合
   I don't want to run in a park **full** of people.（人がいっぱいの公園で走りたくない）

B. その他の注意すべき形容詞：SVOC の C（補語）として使用される

The innovative marketing strategy (S) made (V) the business (O) **profitable** (C).
（革新的なマーケティング戦略がその事業を黒字にした）
*O = C (the business was profitable) の関係が成立しています。

**副詞**

A. 動詞、形容詞、副詞、名詞、数字、句や節、文全体などを修飾する働きがある

1. **副詞**を修飾する　* 副詞の amazingly が副詞の well を修飾しています。
   That treadmill used in gyms sold **amazingly** well.
   （ジムで使用されるそのランニングマシンは驚くほどよく売れた）
2. **数字**を修飾する　*approximately が 5,000 を修飾しています。
   The company employs **approximately** 5,000 people worldwide.
   （その企業は世界中におよそ 5,000 人の人たちを雇用している）
3. **句**や**節**を修飾する　*long が後ろの副詞節を修飾しています。
   We usually reserve hotel rooms **long** before the vacation starts.
   （私たちは通常、休暇が始まるずっと前にホテルの部屋を予約する）

B. -ly の有無で意味が異なる頻出の副詞

late（遅く）/ lately（最近）　hard（一生懸命に）/ hardly（ほとんど～ない）
most（最も）/ mostly（たいてい）　near（近くに）/ nearly（ほとんど）
high（高く）/ highly（大いに）　just（ちょうど）/ justly（正当に）

**間違いやすい副詞と形容詞**

○ The restaurant uses only local vegetables in its (**carefully**) prepared dishes.
× The restaurant uses only local vegetables in its (**careful**) prepared dishes.
（そのレストランは、**丁寧に**調理された料理に地元の野菜のみを使用している）
*prepared（形容詞）を修飾しているので carefully（副詞）が入ります。prepared dishes（惣菜）という名詞のかたまりを修飾する場合は、文脈によって several や frozen などの形容詞が入ることもあります。

## Part 5 Incomplete Sentences

***A word or phrase is missing in each of the sentences below. Choose the best word or phrase to complete the sentence.***

**14.** The meeting was extended by one hour, which made Mr. Jobson -------- for his annual health checkup.
(A) late
(B) later
(C) latest
(D) lately
Ⓐ Ⓑ Ⓒ Ⓓ

**15.** Thanks to the company's health and fitness campaign, employees are now -------- healthier than the previous year.
(A) noticeable
(B) noticeably
(C) notice
(D) noticed
Ⓐ Ⓑ Ⓒ Ⓓ

**16.** Although people may find the aerobics class -------- at first, it offers both physical and mental benefits.
(A) exhaust
(B) exhaustion
(C) exhausting
(D) exhaustingly
Ⓐ Ⓑ Ⓒ Ⓓ

**17.** Your personal trainer at the Blue Sky Fitness Center will design the -------- workout plan to help you achieve your fitness goals.
(A) optimism
(B) optimal
(C) optimally
(D) optimize
Ⓐ Ⓑ Ⓒ Ⓓ

**18.** A lifting belt is an important accessory that provides -------- and protection for your back when lifting heavy weights.
(A) stable
(B) stably
(C) stabilize
(D) stability
Ⓐ Ⓑ Ⓒ Ⓓ

### Study Point Part 6 長文穴埋め問題

このパートでは、Part 5のような、適切な前置詞を選ぶ問題も出されます。短時間で解答できるので、残り時間が少ないときは優先的に解いていきましょう。

1. combine A **with** B ［AをBと組み合わせる］
2. serve **as** A ［Aとして勤務する］
3. enroll **in** A ［Aに登録する］
4. look **up** A ［Aを調べる］
5. attach A **to** B ［AをBに添付する］
6. interview A **for** B ［A（人）にB（仕事など）の面接をする］

## Part 6 Text Completion

***Read a short text. Some words, phrases or sentences are missing from the text. Read the questions and choose the answer to complete the text.***

**Questions 19 to 22** refer to the following letter.

Dear Mr. Rodriguez,

I am writing to congratulate you on reaching retirement age, which means that you are now officially a senior citizen of Oakland City.

Please -------- (**19.**) that, as a senior citizen, you are entitled to a free annual health checkup at Oakland General Hospital. -------- (**20.**) .

To schedule your first checkup, simply contact Oakland General Hospital's appointment desk by telephone at 046-972-5515, and provide them -------- (**21.**) your details.

If you have any questions or require further assistance, please do not -------- (**22.**) to contact me directly by e-mail: jdavis@oakland-city.gov.

Warm regards,

Jennifer Davis

Oakland City Hall

**19.** (A) to note
(B) noting
(C) noted
(D) note
Ⓐ Ⓑ Ⓒ Ⓓ

**20.** (A) I strongly encourage you to undergo this as soon as possible.
(B) The results of your health checkup have been sent by mail.
(C) The city will cover half of the cost of the treatment.
(D) You can take the health checkup every year until retirement age.
Ⓐ Ⓑ Ⓒ Ⓓ

**21.** (A) to
(B) at
(C) for
(D) with
Ⓐ Ⓑ Ⓒ Ⓓ

**22.** (A) continue
(B) burden
(C) hesitate
(D) demand
Ⓐ Ⓑ Ⓒ Ⓓ

## Study Point　Part 7　説明文問題

このパートでも、すべてを読まなければ解けない問題は、実はそう多くはありません。残り時間が少ないときは、次の文言に注目して効率よく解答していきましょう。

例 1）What is the purpose of **the second e-mail**?
→ 2 番目の E-mail だけ を見れば問題が解ける可能性があります。

例 2）**According to the table**, what is the problem?
→ 表だけを見れば問題が解ける可能性があります。

例 3）**In the letter, the word "meet" in paragraph 2, line 3**, is closest in meaning to
→ 手紙の第 2 段落 3 行目を見れば問題が解ける可能性があります。

## Part 7　Double Passages

***Read the text and the questions following the text. Select the best answer for each question.***

**Questions 23 to 27** refer to the following Web page and e-mail.

http://www.FitTechHealth.com/companynews

We are pleased to announce that our latest design, the FitOne, will debut this August and be installed in all FitTech gyms soon after! The FitOne has been developed as an all-in-one exercise machine for a full-body workout. Since November last year, our design team has worked closely with leading fitness experts and engineers to produce a state-of-the-art product. Furthermore, it is made of durable materials, designed to stand up to heavy and prolonged use. The FitOne will always be available when you need it, unlike machines at other gyms, which often have out-of-order signs.

| | |
|---|---|
| To: | Taro Yamashita <t.yamashita@fittech.co.jp> |
| From: | Emily Claymore <emmyc@fastmail.com> |
| Subject: | FitOne region availability |
| Date: | June 22 |

Hi Taro,

I'm very excited about the debut of FitTech's newest fitness machine. I'm contacting you to ask about the availability of the FitOne in the US. I know that the FitOne will debut in Japan first, but as the Eastern US regional manager, I would like more detailed information on the time frame of availability of the FitOne here. Can we still expect it a month after the Japanese release?

We have advertised the FitOne's debut over here, and our customers are really looking forward to using this new piece of equipment. In fact, since your announcement we have seen a 12-percent increase in new members, which is 8 percent higher than our expected membership growth.

Thanks again,

Emily

**23.** What is the purpose of the Web page?
(A) To announce a new product
(B) To introduce new branch locations
(C) To invite feedback about a service
(D) To publicize a successful product Ⓐ Ⓑ Ⓒ Ⓓ

**24.** What is indicated about the FitOne?
(A) It is already available.
(B) It will be manufactured overseas.
(C) It is an advanced product.
(D) It requires special skills to use. Ⓐ Ⓑ Ⓒ Ⓓ

**25.** Why does Ms. Claymore send an e-mail to Mr. Yamashita?
(A) To ask for a product demonstration
(B) To express her disappointment
(C) To find out when she will receive the new product
(D) To inform him of their recent success Ⓐ Ⓑ Ⓒ Ⓓ

**26.** What does the e-mail indicate about the customers' perspective?
(A) They are concerned about the durability of the FitOne.
(B) They are frustrated by unreliable equipment.
(C) They are interested in all-in-one fitness equipment.
(D) They are not aware of the FitOne. Ⓐ Ⓑ Ⓒ Ⓓ

**27.** What is the result of the advertising efforts in the US?
(A) New locations have opened.
(B) Profits have increased.
(C) Equipment has improved.
(D) More members have joined.

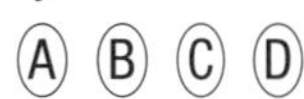

## Review Exercise

***Read this shorter versions of the Web page and e-mail in Part 7. Fill in appropriate words in the blank spaces from the box below***

Our newest creation, the FitOne, is [1]__________ this August to all FitTech gyms! It's an all-in-one exercise machine designed for a full-body [2]__________. Developed since last November, it's a state-of-the-art product made of durable [3]__________. Unlike other gyms' equipment, the FitOne will always be [4]__________ when you need it.

Hi Taro,

I'm [5]__________ about FitTech's new FitOne machine. Can you provide details on [6]__________ it will be available in the Eastern US? Our [7]__________ are eager, and we've already seen a 12% increase in new members [8]__________ the announcement.

Thanks!

| | | | |
|---|---|---|---|
| (a) available | (b) coming | (c) workout | (d) when |
| (e) since | (f) excited | (g) customers | (h) materials |

MEMO

UNIT 09

# IT and Technology

## Vocabulary Exercise

***Match each English word with its meaning in Japanese.***

**1.** questionnaire (　　)　**2.** retail (　　)　**3.** make use of (　　)
**4.** adjacent (　　)　**5.** session (　　)　**6.** address (　　)　**7.** notification (　　)
**8.** proceed (　　)　**9.** delete (　　)　**10.** transfer (　　)

a. 進む　b. 移す、移動させる　c. 集まり、会議　d. 隣接した　e. 利用する
f. 小売りの　g. 話しかける、演説する　h. アンケート　i. 削除する　j. 通知

# LISTENING SECTION

## Dictation Exercise

***Listen to the following sentences. Fill in the blank spaces.***

1. Could you ________________ this device into the power outlet?
2. First, ________________ a new document and then save it in your "Documents" folder.
3. Let's switch off our cell phones. We don't want any ________________ during the meeting.
4. We have invited 100 registered customers to take part in the product ________________ session.
5. After you have ________________ the online questionnaire, please click on the "Submit" button.

**Study Point**　Part 1 写真描写問題

意味のわからない難しい単語が読み上げられたときは、思い切ってその選択肢を一旦除外しましょう。そして残り3つの選択肢に集中して、「すべて当てはまらない」と思ったときだけ、その選択肢を正解に選びましょう。

例）**1.** There are some **water fountains** in a park.
**2.** There are some benches in a garden.
**3.** Some trees are being cut down.
**4.** Some bicycles have been left in a parking area.

⇒ 1の **water fountains**（噴水）の意味がわからないときは、**残り3つの選択肢だけからでも正解できる**と前向きに考えてみましょう。

## Part 1 Photographs

2-02, 03

***Look at the picture and listen to four statements. Choose one statement that best describes the situation in the picture.***

1.

Ⓐ Ⓑ Ⓒ Ⓓ

2.

Ⓐ Ⓑ Ⓒ Ⓓ

### Study Point Part 2 応答問題

**Why ～ ?** と聞かれたら、**Because ...** と答え、**How can ～ ?** であれば、**By ～ ing** 形を使うのが基本的な答え方です。

1. **Why** did you cancel your business trip? – **Because** the conference got postponed.
   (なぜ出張をキャンセルしたのですか ― 会議が延期になったからです)
2. **How can** I get this coupon? – **By** complet**ing** a questionnaire.
   (どうしたらこのクーポンが手に入りますか ― アンケートにすべて答えることによってです)

* ただし、これを逆手にとって **Because ....** や **By ～ ing** 形が**不正解**の選択肢として使われるケースもあります。最後までしっかり聞いて判断しましょう。

## Part 2 Question-Response

CD 2-04〜08

***Listen to a question or statement and three responses. Choose the best response to the question or statement.***

3. Mark your answer on your answer sheet. Ⓐ Ⓑ Ⓒ

4. Mark your answer on your answer sheet. Ⓐ Ⓑ Ⓒ

5. Mark your answer on your answer sheet. Ⓐ Ⓑ Ⓒ

6. Mark your answer on your answer sheet. Ⓐ Ⓑ Ⓒ

7. Mark your answer on your answer sheet. Ⓐ Ⓑ Ⓒ

### Study Point Part 3 会話問題

このパートでは、冒頭で相手の名前を呼びかけたり、社名を名乗ったりすることがよくあります。ですが、選択肢の中に人の名前などが記されていない場合は、**万一その名前を聞き逃してしまっても、解答に支障が出ないこともあります。焦りは禁物です。**

会話の冒頭の例

例 1）Thanks for coming today, **Patricia**.（パトリシア、今日は来てくれて有り難う）

例 2）**Jerome**, is everything OK?（ジェローム、すべて順調ですか）

例 3）**Prashant**, did you see the sales report?（プラシャント、売り上げ報告書を見ましたか）

例 4）Hello, you've reached **Helix PC**.（こんにちは、こちらはヘリックス PC です）

## Part 3 Conversation

***Listen to a conversation between two people. Read the questions on your answer sheet. Choose the best answer for each question.***

**8.** Who most likely is the man?
(A) A salesperson
(B) An IT staff member
(C) The woman's assistant
(D) The woman's customer

Ⓐ Ⓑ Ⓒ Ⓓ

**9.** What does the woman want to finish?
(A) Her candidate interview
(B) Her presentation preparation
(C) Her research
(D) Her team's big task

Ⓐ Ⓑ Ⓒ Ⓓ

**10.** What does the woman mean when she says, "Well, we're going as fast as we can"?
(A) Her team will try to finish their task by the end of the month.
(B) It is not possible to finish the task.
(C) The computer system is running as fast as possible.
(D) Computer problems have delayed the project.

Ⓐ Ⓑ Ⓒ Ⓓ

## Study Point Part 4 説明文問題

このパートでは、話し手が相手に伝えたいことや頼みたいことを列挙する場合があります。最初に **First** という言葉が聞こえたら、以下のようなパターンを想定してみましょう。ちなみに、列挙される数は多くても **3** つくらいです。

例 1）We have a few announcements.（いくつかお知らせがあります）
**First**, ...
**Also**, ...　[ あるいは **Then**,... / **And**, ... / **After that**, ... など ]

例 2）Here are some tips.（いくつかヒントを紹介します）
**First**, ...
**And**, ...
**Finally**, ...

## Part 4 Talk

CD 2-11, 12

***Listen to a talk given by a single speaker. Read the questions on your answer sheet. Choose the best answer for each question.***

**11.** Who is the speaker addressing?
(A) Award winners
(B) Department managers
(C) New employees
(D) Product testers
Ⓐ Ⓑ Ⓒ Ⓓ

**12.** What does the speaker ask the listeners to do?
(A) Fill out a form
(B) Give their opinions about their jobs
(C) Tell their personal stories
(D) Write a report on their departments
Ⓐ Ⓑ Ⓒ Ⓓ

**13.** What will listeners receive later?
(A) An award
(B) A coupon
(C) An evaluation
(D) An application form
Ⓐ Ⓑ Ⓒ Ⓓ

# READING SECTION

## Study Point Part 5 短文穴埋め問題

### 関係代名詞／関係副詞／複合関係代名詞

（※疑問代名詞は関係代名詞とは文法的に異なるものですが、よく出題されるのであわせて紹介しておきます。）

**which**

① **関係代名詞（非制限用法：先行詞の補足説明をする）**

TechStar Software, **which** recently changed ownership, is performing well.
（TechStar Software は最近所有者が代わったが、業績を伸ばしている）

* 先行詞が特定のものや固有名詞の場合は、which の前にカンマがついて非制限用法になります。

② **疑問代名詞（「どちらの、どの」という意味を表す）**

The shop has not yet decided **which** computers to feature during the sale.
（その店はセール期間中にどのコンピューターを目玉にするかまだ決めていない）

* 疑問代名詞の which は名詞の前に置いて形容詞的に使うことができます。

**whose**

① **関係代名詞（制限用法：先行詞を明確にする）**

We would like to thank employees **whose** contributions are greatly acknowledged.（私たちは、その貢献が大いに認められる従業員たちに感謝したい）

* 先行詞が不特定の人や物の場合、whose の前にカンマがない**制限用法**になります。

② **疑問代名詞（「誰の」という意味を表す）**

The staff does not know **whose** pen was left behind in the meeting room.
（誰のペンが会議室に置き忘れられていたのかスタッフにはわからない）

**when**

① **関係副詞（非制限用法：先行詞の補足説明をする）**

His business trip will begin next Friday, **when** he attends a seminar on AI.
（彼の出張は次の金曜日からで、その日に彼は AI に関するセミナーに出席する）

② **関係副詞（制限用法：先行詞を明確にする）**

I hope the time will soon come **when** we will be able to travel to the moon.
（私たちが月に旅行できる時が早く来ることを願っています）

* この文のように先行詞（the time）と when が離れることもあるので注意しましょう。

**whoever（複合関係代名詞）**

① **名詞節を作る：「〜する人は誰でも（= anyone who）」**

A prize will be awarded to **whoever** solves the mystery first.
（最初にその謎を解いた人は誰であれ、賞が与えられる）

***Whoever** wants to join is welcome.（参加したい人は誰でも歓迎します）のように主語になることもできます。

② **副詞節を作る：「だれが（を）〜しようとも（= no matter who）」**

**Whoever** is elected mayor, it will be difficult to solve the problem.
（誰が市長に選ばれても、その問題を解決するのは困難だろう）

## Part 5 Incomplete Sentences

***A word or phrase is missing in each of the sentences below. Choose the best word or phrase to complete the sentence.***

**14.** This e-mail is being sent to all staff members -------- passwords for the computer system have not yet been changed.
(A) who
(B) whom
(C) whose
(D) whoever
Ⓐ Ⓑ Ⓒ Ⓓ

**15.** As a part of the IT survey, employees were asked to indicate -------- software programs they used most often.
(A) when
(B) why
(C) where
(D) which
Ⓐ Ⓑ Ⓒ Ⓓ

**16.** We should offer training on the new software to -------- needs it so that its introduction can go smoothly.
(A) anyone
(B) what
(C) whoever
(D) those
Ⓐ Ⓑ Ⓒ Ⓓ

**17.** TitanTech's products will be available for purchase from next Monday, -------- its new Web site goes online.
(A) when
(B) as for
(C) instead
(D) by which
Ⓐ Ⓑ Ⓒ Ⓓ

**18.** This tablet can be used for a whole day on one charge, -------- it is best to bring a portable battery just in case.
(A) once
(B) since
(C) although
(D) when
Ⓐ Ⓑ Ⓒ Ⓓ

### Study Point Part 6 長文穴埋め問題

今回は、よく登場する群前置詞（複数の語が集まって１つの前置詞と同じ働きをするもの）を紹介します。知っていないと正解できないものばかりなので、すべて覚えましょう。

**1. in charge of ~** [～を担当して]
**2. on behalf of ~** [～に代わって]
**3. in addition to ~** [～に加えて]
**4. prior to ~** [～より前に]
**5. as of ~** [～の時点で]
**6. regardless of ~** [～にかかわらず]
**7. in regard to ~** [～に関して]

## Part 6 Text Completion

***Read a short text. Some words, phrases or sentences are missing from the text. Read the questions and choose the answer to complete the text.***

**Questions 19 to 22** refer to the following article.

Retail giant Blazing announced a new concept in grocery stores, ------- (19.) Blazing to Go, at a press conference yesterday. These new stores have no queues or checkout counters. ------- (20.) to Gregory Newsome, Blazing's CEO, these stores make use of scanning technology on users' smartphones. Shoppers just download the app, walk into any Blazing to Go store, and pick ------- (21.) they want off the shelves. ------- (22.). The bill is paid for on the Blazing account monthly. There is no waiting in line, no need to use a cashier, and no waiting for change.

**19.** (A) call
(B) calls
(C) called
(D) calling
Ⓐ Ⓑ Ⓒ Ⓓ

**20.** (A) According
(B) Contrary
(C) Parallel
(D) Similar
Ⓐ Ⓑ Ⓒ Ⓓ

**21.** (A) on
(B) that
(C) what
(D) up
Ⓐ Ⓑ Ⓒ Ⓓ

**22.** (A) After you check out, you can have your items delivered.
(B) Special software is not needed to shop at the stores.
(C) The item is scanned and added to a bill automatically.
(D) When the item is sold out, you will get a notification.
Ⓐ Ⓑ Ⓒ Ⓓ

**Study Point** Part 7 読解問題

TOEIC L&R TEST では、メールやメモを扱う場合、本文の前に**ヘッダー**と呼ばれる部分が表示されます。以下の 5 つを理解して、そのメールやメモは**誰から誰に宛てたものなのか**などをしっかり確認した上で、本文を読み進めていきましょう。

| | |
|---|---|
| To : | ← 宛先 |
| From: | ← 差出人 |
| Date: | ← 日付 |
| Subject: | ← 件名（Re: と表記されることもあります。ただし、"Subject: Re: Question" など書かれていたら、その Re は**返信**を意味します） |
| Attachment: | ← 添付ファイル（この欄はないことの方が多いです） |

## Part 7 Double Passages

***Read the text and the questions following the text. Select the best answer for each question.***

**Questions 23 to 27** refer to the following memo and e-mail.

**MEMO**

To: All Employees
From: IT Department
Date: July 28
Subject: New Office E-mail System

Please be aware that the installation date of the new office e-mail software is imminent.

As mentioned in our announcement last month, the new software will be installed on Saturday, August 1. According to the installation schedule, it will be ready to use on the Monday after that.

Please remember that your e-mails on the old system will not be automatically transferred to the new system. If you have any important e-mails, you need to save them to your cloud drive or PC hard disk by the end of July. Please note that if your cloud drive has a lot of files, it may be near the storage limit. In that case, delete some files on the cloud drive, or else just save your e-mails to your local hard disk. If you have any questions or problems, please contact Susan Wilson in the IT Department, extension 526.

| | |
|---|---|
| To: | IT Department |
| From: | Martin Bartosz |
| Date: | July 29 |
| Subject: | New E-mail System |

Hello. This is Martin Bartosz in Sales. Regarding the new e-mail system, I have been trying to save my important mails from the old system to my cloud drive but I get an error message every time. Please advise me on how to proceed. Also, do I need to make a new password for the new system, or can I continue to use my current password?

Regards,
Martin Bartosz

**23.** Why did the IT Department send the memo?
(A) To announce a change
(B) To remind employees
(C) To obtain feedback
(D) To ask for opinions
Ⓐ Ⓑ Ⓒ Ⓓ

**24.** In the memo, the word "imminent" in paragraph 1, line 2, is closest in meaning to
(A) forthcoming
(B) important
(C) decided
(D) adjacent
Ⓐ Ⓑ Ⓒ Ⓓ

**25.** What is indicated about the new office e-mail system?
(A) It has already been installed.
(B) It will allow users to read old e-mails.
(C) It can be accessed from August 3.
(D) It requires a PC upgrade.
Ⓐ Ⓑ Ⓒ Ⓓ

**26.** According to the information in the memo, what most likely is the cause of Mr. Bartosz's problem?
(A) He forgot his computer password.
(B) He saved files to his local hard drive.
(C) He deleted files on his cloud drive.
(D) His cloud drive is nearly full.
Ⓐ Ⓑ Ⓒ Ⓓ

**27.** In the e-mail, what does Mr. Bartosz ask about?
(A) Software upgrades
(B) File permissions
(C) Login procedures
(D) Antivirus measures
Ⓐ Ⓑ Ⓒ Ⓓ

## Review Exercise

***Read this shorter versions of the memo and e-mail in Part 7. Fill in appropriate words in the blank spaces from the box below.***

The new office e-mail software will be [1]__________ on Saturday, August 1st, and will be operational by the following Monday. Please back up any [2]__________ e-mails from the old system to your cloud drive or PC hard disk by [3]__________ July, as e-mails will not be transferred [4]_____________. Check your cloud storage [5]_____________ and clear space if needed, or save the e-mails locally on your PC.

Hello. I'm having [6]__________ transferring my e-mails to my cloud drive due to error [7]__________. Can you advise on what to do? Also, do I need to create a new password for the new e-mail system or can I use my [8]__________ one?

| | | | |
|---|---|---|---|
| (a) important | (b) capacity | (c) automatically | (d) current |
| (e) trouble | (f) the end of | (g) messages | (h) installed |

MEMO

UNIT 10

# Shopping

## Vocabulary Exercise

*Match each English word with its meaning in Japanese.*

**1.** spokesperson (　　)　**2.** in line (　　)　**3.** neighborhood (　　)
**4.** fabric (　　)　**5.** sidewalk (　　)　**6.** attach (　　)　**7.** merchandise (　　)
**8.** boost (　　)　**9.** range (　　)　**10.** stop in (　　)

a. 添付する　b. 商品　c. 一列になって　d. 立ち寄る　e. 及ぶ
f. 歩道　g. 広報担当者　h. 近隣　i. 増やす、後押しする　j. 布地

# LISTENING SECTION

## Dictation Exercise

CD 2-13

*Listen to the following sentences. Fill in the blank spaces.*

1. If you wish to leave your ________________ here, please attach a name tag to each item.
2. The new EclipsePro smartphone is ____________ to a depth of three meters.
3. After opening the front door, the first thing to notice is the beautiful ________ .
4. The on-campus branch of Maxwell is known for the ____________ stationery prices in town.
5. ______________ from all over Keston County attended the harvest festival last weekend.

**Study Point** Part 1 写真描写問題

ものが主語の時には**現在完了形**が使われます。現在完了形がいきなり登場すると戸惑うかもしれませんが、〈**have[has] been +過去分詞**〉で「**〜された状態である**」という意味なので、実は現在形とほとんど変わりません。

例）**1.** A cup **has been left** on top of magazines.
（カップが雑誌の上に置かれたままになっている）
**2.** Shopping carts **have been placed** together.
（ショッピングカートがまとめて置かれている）
**3.** Chairs **have been stacked** against a wall.
（椅子が壁際に積み重ねられている）
**4.** A big screen **has been installed** in a room.
（大きなスクリーンが部屋に設置されている）
**5.** Boxes **have been scattered** on the ground.（箱が地面に散らばっている）

## Part 1 》Photographs

***Look at the picture and listen to four statements. Choose one statement that best describes the situation in the picture.***

1.

2.

Ⓐ Ⓑ Ⓒ Ⓓ

### Study Point　Part 2 応答問題

Unit 3 で、肯定文の文末に **right?** を付けて「～ですよね」と確認する形について説明しました。今回はそれと似た形の**付加疑問文**を紹介します。

例）

1. The copy machine is being fixed today, **isn't it?** − No, not until next week.
（コピー機は今日、修理されているのですよね？ーいいえ、来週まではされません）
2. You've been to this museum before, **haven't you?** − No, I haven't.
（あなたは以前にこの博物館に来たことがありますよね？ーいいえ、ありません）
3. You didn't cancel the reservation, **did you?** − No, did you want me to?
（あなたはその予約をキャンセルしなかったですよね？ーしてません。私にそうしてほしかったのですか）　* **否定文**には**肯定の付加疑問文**が付くので注意が必要です。

## Part 2 Question-Response

*Listen to a question or statement and three responses. Choose the best response to the question or statement.*

3. Mark your answer on your answer sheet. Ⓐ Ⓑ Ⓒ
4. Mark your answer on your answer sheet. Ⓐ Ⓑ Ⓒ
5. Mark your answer on your answer sheet. Ⓐ Ⓑ Ⓒ
6. Mark your answer on your answer sheet. Ⓐ Ⓑ Ⓒ
7. Mark your answer on your answer sheet. Ⓐ Ⓑ Ⓒ

### Study Point Part 3 会話問題

このパートでは、会話をしている場所について聞かれることがよくあります。質問パターンは大きく分けると以下の3つで、選択肢には **In a restaurant** や **At the station** などの短い選択肢が並びます。

1. Where most likely are the speakers?
（話し手たちはどこにいると考えられますか）
2. Where does the conversation most likely take place?
（会話はどこで行われていると考えられますか）
3. Where is the conversation most likely taking place?
（会話はどこで行われているところだと考えられますか）

## Part 3 Conversation

*Listen to a conversation between two people. Read the questions on your answer sheet. Choose the best answer for each question.*

8. Where most likely are the speakers?
(A) At a furniture store
(B) At a garden store
(C) At a shoe store
(D) At an office supply store
Ⓐ Ⓑ Ⓒ Ⓓ

9. Who is the man shopping for?
(A) Himself
(B) His daughter
(C) His wife
(D) His wife's father Ⓐ Ⓑ Ⓒ Ⓓ

10. What does the woman imply when she says, "Oh, I've got it!"?
(A) She found a good price on an item.
(B) She has the man's address.
(C) She remembered an item for the man.
(D) She thought of a new plan to help the man. Ⓐ Ⓑ Ⓒ Ⓓ

## Study Point　Part 4 説明文問題

疑問文の中に〈動詞+（助）動詞〉の形があると、混乱してしまうことがあるかもしれません。事前によく理解しておきましょう。

例）

**1. What does the speaker say is discounted?**

（話し手は、何が割り引きになっていると言っていますか）

*What does the speaker say ∧ is discounted?

（ここにあった what が文頭に移動したと考えましょう）

**2. What does the speaker say will be discussed at the meeting?**

（話し手は、会議で何について話し合われるだろうと言っていますか）

*What does the speaker say ∧ will be discussed at the meeting?

（ここにあった what が文頭に移動したと考えましょう）

## Part 4 Talk

***Listen to a talk given by a single speaker. Read the questions on your answer sheet. Choose the best answer for each question.***

**11.** What does the speaker say is unique about the store?
(A) It has the largest parking area.
(B) It has the lowest prices.
(C) It offers the most variety of bread.
(D) It provides services for customers' cars.　Ⓐ Ⓑ Ⓒ Ⓓ

**12.** What can a customer get on sale this week at Redburn?
(A) Chicken legs
(B) Fish
(C) Ground beef
(D) Yogurt　Ⓐ Ⓑ Ⓒ Ⓓ

**13.** What is new at the Harrison neighborhood store?
(A) A dining section
(B) A larger meat section
(C) Faster check-out lanes
(D) More choices of vegetables　Ⓐ Ⓑ Ⓒ Ⓓ

# READING SECTION

## Study Point Part 5 短文穴埋め問題

### 比較

**比較級**

① He is **more interested** in online shopping than in conventional shopping.
（彼は従来の買い物よりもオンライン・ショッピングに興味を持っている）
*than の後ろの in は be interested in の in で省略することもできます。

② She became progressively **better** at understanding the needs of customers.
（彼女は顧客のニーズを理解するのが次第にうまくなった）
***be(become) good at ~ing** ＝「～することがうまい（うまくなる）」

③ Many retail shops place **more emphasis** on online shopping.
（多くの小売店はオンライン・ショッピングを重視している）
***place emphasis on A** は「A を重視する」という意味の頻出熟語です。

④ The company aims to make computers **more accessible** to everyone.
（その企業は、コンピューターが誰にとってもより身近なものになることを目指している）
*〈**make ＋名詞＋ more ＋形容詞**〉＝「**（名詞）をより～にする**」

**最上級**

① He purchased **the narrowest** of all the bookcases sold in that furniture store.
（彼は、その家具店で売られているすべての本棚の中で一番幅の狭いものを購入した）
*〈**the ＋形容詞の最上級＋ of all the ＋複数名詞**〉＝「**すべての～の中で最も…なもの**」

② EastPark Center is **the third largest** shopping mall in Los Angeles.
（イーストパーク・センターはロサンゼルスで 3 番目に大きなショッピングモールだ）
*the と最上級の間に**序数詞（second, fourth, fifth など）**が入ります。

**far の比較級**

① The electric car can go **farther** on one charge than any other electric car.
（その電気自動車は、1 回の充電で他のどの電気自動車よりも遠くまで走ることができる）
***farther** ＝「**（距離に関して）より遠く**」。最上級は **farthest** です。

② The food situation in developing countries was **further** complicated by global warming.
（発展途上国の食糧事情は、地球温暖化によっていっそう複雑になった）
***further** ＝「**（程度に関して）いっそう**」。最上級は **furthest** です。

**その他の比較表現**

- Many shoppers like to buy groceries in the suburbs **rather than** in the center of the city.
（多くの買い物客は、市の中心部ではなく郊外で食料雑貨類を買うことを好む）
***A rather than B** ＝「B ではなくむしろ A」

## Part 5 Incomplete Sentences

***A word or phrase is missing in each of the sentences below. Choose the best word or phrase to complete the sentence.***

**14.** Among all the sample designs we have received for our shop's new logo, this one is the -------- .
(A) bold
(B) bolder
(C) boldest
(D) boldly
Ⓐ Ⓑ Ⓒ Ⓓ

**15.** At present, retail giant Bentrose Ltd. is focusing on its domestic customers -------- making efforts to enter international markets.
(A) in contrast
(B) by means of
(C) rather than
(D) after all
Ⓐ Ⓑ Ⓒ Ⓓ

**16.** Lantos Supermarket seems to be -------- about the quality of its products than the number of new customers.
(A) concerned
(B) too concerned
(C) more concerned
(D) most concerned
Ⓐ Ⓑ Ⓒ Ⓓ

**17.** By accessing the store's Web site, customers can ------- browse and purchase products online.
(A) easy
(B) easily
(C) easier
(D) easiest
Ⓐ Ⓑ Ⓒ Ⓓ

**18.** The budget for advertising was -------- increased to boost in-store sales in the first quarter.
(A) further
(B) lots
(C) rather than
(D) instead of
Ⓐ Ⓑ Ⓒ Ⓓ

### Study Point Part 6 長文穴埋め問題

空所に入る**1**文を選択する問題では、空所の直後に意味のわかりにくい、文と文をつなぐ副詞（句）があると、正解に辿り着くのが難しくなります。しっかりおさらいしておきましょう。

1. **on the contrary** [ それとは反対に ]
2. **otherwise** [ そうでなければ ]
3. **as such** [ そのため、従って ]
4. **moreover** [ さらに、なおまた ]
5. **consequently** [ その結果として ]
6. **meanwhile** [ その間に ]

## Part 6 Text Completion

***Read a short text. Some words, phrases or sentences are missing from the text. Read the questions and choose the answer to complete the text.***

**Questions 19 to 22** refer to the following article.

A collection of over 100 dazzling golden items is on display at the Golden Exhibit on the top floor of Gregory's Department Store in Blairsville. -------(**19.**) have been delighted at the shiny pieces, which range in size from small nuggets of raw gold to statues of golden animals. A spokesperson for Gregory's says the public response has been -------(**20.**) positive that they are considering making it an annual event.

Two of the items, a large bowl made of pure gold and a matching cup, -------(**21.**) to be extremely valuable. -------(**22.**) . As such, security has been a priority for the store, and an extra team of guards has been hired for round-the-clock protection.

**19.** (A) Diners
(B) Members
(C) Participants
(D) Visitors
Ⓐ Ⓑ Ⓒ Ⓓ

**20.** (A) much
(B) so
(C) such
(D) that
Ⓐ Ⓑ Ⓒ Ⓓ

**21.** (A) is said
(B) are said
(C) is saying
(D) are saying
Ⓐ Ⓑ Ⓒ Ⓓ

**22.** (A) On May 7, the exhibit will be packed up and moved to nearby Middleton.
(B) The collection as a whole is estimated to be worth over a million dollars.
(C) That is why they are not included in this exhibition.
(D) The store's security team has been doing a great job guarding the items.
Ⓐ Ⓑ Ⓒ Ⓓ

## Study Point Part 7 読解問題

図表は設問内容を推測する際のヒントになることがあります。一番上に何が書かれているか注目しましょう。

タイトル例）

1. Art Online Supply Store Order Form
   ⇒ 美術用具のオンライン注文票であることがわかります。
2. Airport Shuttle Bus schedule
   ⇒ 空港シャトルバスの時刻表であることがわかります。
3. Sales Figures for Last Month
   ⇒ 先月の売上高であることがわかります。
4. Itinerary for David Waldman
   ⇒ David Waldman さんの旅程表であることがわかります。

## Part 7 Double Passages

***Read the text and the questions following the text. Select the best answer for each question.***

**Questions 23 to 27** refer to the following e-mail and table.

| | |
|---|---|
| To: | All staff |
| From: | James & Sons Supermarket Head Office |
| Date: | October 1 |
| Subject: | Sales of vegetables |
| Attachment: | Oct.Sales.Data |

Dear Staff,

Thank you for all your recent efforts. The "Harvest Festival" sales campaign last month was a great success.

This month we are aiming to increase sales of the following items: pumpkins, butternut squash, celery, cauliflower and turnips. The data for the October sales last year for these vegetables are attached to this e-mail. As you may remember, turnip sales were low due to the bad weather and poor harvest. Farmers are telling us that the weather has been ideal this year and so we are expecting good sales.

We will be discounting the two items that had the lowest sales last year. Please emphasize these discounts on the displays in stores.

Our predicted sales for October this year are indicated on the right. To help boost sales of pumpkins, we will be offering a free color recipe for pumpkin pie and frozen pie pastry at a 50 percent discount to customers who buy it together with a pumpkin.

## October Sales Data

| | Last Year | This Year (forecast) |
|---|---|---|
| Pumpkins | 220 | (400) |
| Butternut squash | 44 | (60) |
| Celery | 79 | (100) |
| Cauliflowers | 188 | (200) |
| Turnips | 23 | (50) |

(figures in 100s of dollars)

**23.** What is indicated about recent sales?
(A) They have been successful.
(B) The head office is disappointed.
(C) The data will be available soon.
(D) A new product sold well.
Ⓐ Ⓑ Ⓒ Ⓓ

**24.** In the e-mail, the word "efforts" in paragraph 1, line 1, is closest in meaning to
(A) discussions
(B) hard work
(C) good advice
(D) rewards
Ⓐ Ⓑ Ⓒ Ⓓ

**25.** What has been confirmed about turnips this year?
(A) A new flavor
(B) Bigger sizes
(C) A price increase
(D) A good harvest
Ⓐ Ⓑ Ⓒ Ⓓ

**26.** Which items will have special displays?
(A) Butternut squash and turnips
(B) Pumpkins and cauliflowers
(C) Celery and turnips
(D) Butternut squash and cauliflowers
Ⓐ Ⓑ Ⓒ Ⓓ

**27.** Which item's sales are expected to more than double this year?
(A) Pumpkins
(B) Celery
(C) Cauliflowers
(D) Turnips
Ⓐ Ⓑ Ⓒ Ⓓ

## Review Exercise

***Read this shorter version of the e-mail in Part 7. Fill in appropriate words in the blank spaces from the box below.***

Thank you all for your [1]__________. Last month's "Harvest Festival" sales campaign went very [2]__________.

This month, we want to sell more pumpkins, butternut squash, celery, cauliflower, and turnips. We have attached the [3]__________ data for these from last October. Turnip sales were low last year due to the bad weather, but this year, farmers say it is all [4]__________, so we expect better sales.

We will be discounting the two items that did not sell well last year. Please [5]__________ these discounts in stores.

Our predicted sales for October are shown on the right. To [6]__________ pumpkin sales, we will offer a [7]__________ pumpkin pie recipe and 50 percent off frozen pie pastry to customers who buy [8]__________ a pumpkin and the pastry together.

| | | | |
|---|---|---|---|
| (a) hard work | (b) free | (c) both | (d) well |
| (e) boost | (f) sales | (g) clear | (h) highlight |

MEMO

UNIT 11

# Advertising

## Vocabulary Exercise

***Match each English word with its meaning in Japanese.***

**1.** currently (　　) **2.** register (　　) **3.** impressive (　　) **4.** drop by (　　)
**5.** distribute (　　) **6.** proof (　　) **7.** eligible (　　) **8.** cutting-edge (　　)
**9.** promptly (　　) **10.** feature (　　)

a. 資格のある　b. 証拠、証明　c. 呼び物にする　d. 印象的な　e. 即座に
f. 最先端の　g. ひょっこり立ち寄る　h. 現在　i. 配布する　j. 登録する

# LISTENING SECTION

## Dictation Exercise

***Listen to the following sentences. Fill in the blank spaces.***

1. The best way to promote our new product is by means of an impressive ____________ .
2. I like ____________ on TV that feature music from my favorite band.
3. The IT Department is ____________ on system updates, so computer security is a concern.
4. This new tablet is a great ____________ . Look... it has a 20 percent discount.
5. Enter the competition to have a chance to win $1 million! That's ____________ ! $1 million!

**Study Point** Part 1 写真描写問題

今回のテーマとなっている広告・宣伝は、TOEIC L&R TEST でもよく登場しますが、中には見慣れない単語もあるかもしれません。整理しておきましょう。

**advertisement：**広告（ポスターや看板などの広告媒体そのものを指します）
**poster：**ポスター、張り紙
**billboard：**広告掲示板（通例、屋外にある大きな看板を指します）
**flyer：**ちらし、ビラ
**pamphlet：**パンフレット、小冊子
**brochure：**パンフレット、小冊子
　*flyer は一枚ものなのに対して、pamphlet と brochure は複数ページからなります。

## Part 1 ›› Photographs

 2-26, 27

***Look at the picture and listen to four statements. Choose one statement that best describes the situation in the picture.***

1.

Ⓐ Ⓑ Ⓒ Ⓓ

2.

Ⓐ Ⓑ Ⓒ Ⓓ

**Study Point** Part 2 応答問題

**How** や **When** を使った問いかけに数字で答えるパターンはよくありますが、**What** でもそれは頻繁に起こります。中でも代表的なのが、**What time is it now?** かもしれませんが、他にはどのようなものがあるでしょうか。以下を参考にしてください。

例)

1. What's the **price** of the item?（その商品の値段はいくらですか）
2. What does it **cost** to rent a car?（車を借りるのにいくらかかりますか）
3. What's the **budget** for this project?（このプロジェクトの予算はいくらですか）
4. What's the **date** of the next meeting?（次の会議は何日ですか）
5. What workshop **date** would be best for you?
（ワークショップの日程はいつが一番よいですか）

## Part 2 Question-Response

2-28～32

*Listen to a question or statement and three responses. Choose the best response to the question or statement.*

3. Mark your answer on your answer sheet. Ⓐ Ⓑ Ⓒ
4. Mark your answer on your answer sheet. Ⓐ Ⓑ Ⓒ
5. Mark your answer on your answer sheet. Ⓐ Ⓑ Ⓒ
6. Mark your answer on your answer sheet. Ⓐ Ⓑ Ⓒ
7. Mark your answer on your answer sheet. Ⓐ Ⓑ Ⓒ

### Study Point Part 3 会話問題

話のきっかけとして会話の始めで、**I'm wondering if ～.** や **I was wondering when ～.** などが登場することがあります。少しわかりにくい表現なので、確認してください。

1. **I'm wondering if** you sell running shoes.（ランニングシューズを売っていますか）
「"Do you sell running shoes?" という点について知りたいと**思っている**のですが（どうでしょうか）」という控えめなニュアンスになります。
2. **I was wondering when** it will be updated.（それはいつ更新されますか）
こちらも「"When will it be updated?" という点について知りたいと**思っていた**のですが（どうでしょうか）」という控えめなニュアンスになります。過去形を使っていますが、**現在**のことを言っています。

## Part 3 Conversation

2-33, 34

*Listen to a conversation between two people. Read the questions on your answer sheet. Choose the best answer for each question.*

8. What does the man say is the cause of the delay?
(A) Bad weather
(B) Lack of supplies
(C) Heavy workload
(D) Staffing problems Ⓐ Ⓑ Ⓒ Ⓓ

9. What will the man do next?
(A) Change the flyer design
(B) Contact the company
(C) Order new equipment
(D) Wait until next week
Ⓐ Ⓑ Ⓒ Ⓓ

10. What does the woman suggest?
(A) Going to the printing company in person
(B) Printing the flyers themselves
(C) Using a different printing company
(D) Sending orders more promptly
Ⓐ Ⓑ Ⓒ Ⓓ

**Study Point** **Part 4 説明文問題**

このパートでは次のような設問が出されます。

Q12. What does the speaker mean when she says, **"But you'd better be quick"**?

☝この部分です

下線部分はトークのどこかで必ず登場します。事前にしっかり確認しておきましょう。

## Part 4 Talk

***Listen to a talk given by a single speaker. Read the questions on your answer sheet. Choose the best answer for each question.***

**11.** What is being advertised?
(A) Stationery
(B) IT equipment
(C) Furniture
(D) Clothing
Ⓐ Ⓑ Ⓒ Ⓓ

**12.** What does the speaker mean when he says, "But you'd better be quick"?
(A) The discount is for a limited time only.
(B) The store is closing soon.
(C) Most of the products are already sold.
(D) The deadline is today.
Ⓐ Ⓑ Ⓒ Ⓓ

**13.** How can listeners receive a complimentary item?
(A) By spending a certain amount
(B) By applying for a credit card
(C) By entering a lottery
(D) By buying a set of items
Ⓐ Ⓑ Ⓒ Ⓓ

# READING SECTION

## Study Point Part 5 短文穴埋め問題

### 分詞構文

**付帯状況を表す分詞構文**

① **動作が同時に起きている場合：「～しながら」**

The data were effortlessly analyzed **using** state-of-the-art software.
（そのデータは最先端のソフトウェアを使って難なく分析された）
*「データの分析」と「最先端のソフトウェアの使用」が同時に行われています。

② **動作が引き続いて起きている場合：「～して、そして…」**

**Taking** out a key from her bag, she handed it over to her mother.
（彼女は鞄から鍵を取り出して、母親に手渡した）
*= She took out a key from her bag **and** (she) handed it over to her mother.
☞ 分詞構文の中で最もよく使用されるのは**付帯状況**です。この他に、**時 (when)** ／**原因・理由 (because)** ／**譲歩 (though)** ／**条件 (if)** を表すことができます。

**with ＋独立分詞構文**

On a busy Saturday morning, we saw a line of people waiting to enter the café, **with** many **saying** that they come every week. [ From Unit 3 : Part 6 ]
（忙しい土曜日の朝、私たちはそのカフェに入店待ちの列ができていているのを目にした。そして多くの人が毎週来ていると話した）
* 〈**with ＋目的語＋分詞**〉で**付帯状況**を表します。辞書には**「～しながら」**と書かれていますが、うまく訳せないときは、前から訳していって、with の部分を**「～して、そして」**としてみましょう。また同じ形で**「～なので」**（状況的理由）を表すこともあります。

**慣用的な分詞構文**

① June's sales figures were surprisingly high **given** the poor weather conditions during that month.
（6 月の売上高は、その月の悪天候を考慮すると驚くほど高かった）

② **Given** that the promotion period was just two weeks, the sales were more than expected.
（プロモーション期間がわずか 2 週間だったことを考慮すれば、売り上げは予想以上だった）
* 〈**given ＋名詞**〉と〈**given ＋ that 節**〉の両方があります。

③ **Depending on** how the product is advertised, customers will perceive its value differently.
（商品がどのように宣伝されるかによって、顧客によるその価値の認識は異なる）

④ **Based on** her experience and insight, she was appointed as the project leader. （その経験と見識に基づいて、彼女はプロジェクト・リーダーに任命された）

⑤ **Beginning** on April 1, the Sunday lunch menu will be offered on Saturdays as well.（4 月 1 日から日曜日のランチメニューが土曜日にも提供される）

☞ これらの分詞構文は慣用的に使用されるものです。分詞の意味上の主語と文の主語が異なっていても、分詞の前に意味上の主語は置かれません。

## Part 5 Incomplete Sentences

***A word or phrase is missing in each of the sentences below. Choose the best word or phrase to complete the sentence.***

**14.** We chose Wicks Associates to create our new advertising campaign, -------- the quality and originality of their proposal.
(A) beginning on
(B) given that
(C) depending on
(D) based on
Ⓐ Ⓑ Ⓒ Ⓓ

**15.** Rather than pay for an expensive advertising service, we saved money -------- our posters in-house.
(A) make
(B) made
(C) making
(D) makes
Ⓐ Ⓑ Ⓒ Ⓓ

**16.** The promotion campaign was considered a success, -------- products sold out in stores around the country.
(A) of
(B) with
(C) at
(D) which
Ⓐ Ⓑ Ⓒ Ⓓ

**17.** -------- on June 11, the commercial for Kestrel's new sports utility vehicle will be shown on Channel 3 daily.
(A) Beginning
(B) Following
(C) Succeeding
(D) Resulting
Ⓐ Ⓑ Ⓒ Ⓓ

**18.** -------- that smartphone usage is increasing, companies should focus on Internet and social media advertising.
(A) Taken
(B) Spoken
(C) Given
(D) Chosen
Ⓐ Ⓑ Ⓒ Ⓓ

### Study Point Part 6 長文穴埋め問題

前の文の内容を受けて、〈**That's ＋関係副詞など**〉から始める言い方にはいくつか種類があります。整理しておきましょう。

1. She goes to a gym regularly. **That's how** she stays healthy.
（彼女は定期的にジムに通っています。**そうやって**彼女は健康を維持しています）
2. She is a vegetarian. **That's why** she doesn't eat meat.
（彼女はベジタリアンです。**だから**彼女は肉を食べない**のです**）
3. She doesn't eat meat. **That's because** she is a vegetarian.
（彼女は肉を食べません。**それは**彼女がベジタリアン**だからです**）
4. "Are you sure I said that?" – "**That's what** you said."
「私がそれを言ったというのは確かですか」「あなたはそう言いました」

* how, why = 関係副詞　because = 従属接続詞　what = 関係代名詞

## Part 6 Text Completion

***Read a short text. Some words, phrases or sentences are missing from the text. Read the questions and choose the answer to complete the text.***

**Questions 19 to 22** refer to the following advertisement.

### Soy Meat

Many consumers doubt that soy meat products can taste like real meat.

Here at Eco-Protein, we understand that.

That's ------- **19.** we are offering a free trial for any of our products.

Simply register your personal ------- **20.** on our Web site, choose a soy meat product that you would like to try, and we will then ------- **21.** you a free sample of your choice.

That's right! You can try it – at no cost!

------- **22.** .

**19.** (A) how
(B) why
(C) what
(D) when
Ⓐ Ⓑ Ⓒ Ⓓ

**20.** (A) effects
(B) orders
(C) details
(D) affairs
Ⓐ Ⓑ Ⓒ Ⓓ

**21.** (A) send
(B) sending
(C) sent
(D) to send
Ⓐ Ⓑ Ⓒ Ⓓ

**22.** (A) Payment options include credit card and bank transfer.
(B) You will also receive a coupon to use for future purchases.
(C) After that, we will refund your money as soon as possible.
(D) Thanks to your feedback, we can improve our products.
Ⓐ Ⓑ Ⓒ Ⓓ

**Study Point** Part 7 読解問題

2つまたは3つの文書を扱う設問では、質問の冒頭に"**According to the notice**"などの文言が入ることがあります。限られた時間の中で、その notice がどの文書を指すのかを瞬時に判断できないことがあるかもしれません。そんなときは以下を参考にしましょう。

〔2つの文書〕 Questions 23 to 27 refer to the following **article** and **advertisement**.
⇒ 最初の文書が **article** で、その次が **advertisement** だと判断できます。

〔3つの文書〕 Questions 23 to 27 refer to the following **notice**, **Web page**, and **online form**.
⇒ 最初の文書が **notice** で、次が **Web page**、そして最後が **online form** だと判断できます。

〔3つの文書〕 Questions 23 to 27 refer to the following **agenda** and **e-mails**.
⇒ 最初の文書が **agenda** で、残りの2つが **e-mail** だと判断できます。

## Part 7 Double Passages

***Read the text and the questions following the text. Select the best answer for each question.***

**Questions 23 to 27** refer to the following advertisement and Web page.

### PrimeWave – Smartphone for the Future

Buy the PrimeWave 8 smartphone between October 1 and 31 to get a fantastic offer.

The PrimeWave 8 features cutting-edge technology, including:

- an ultra-fast Zephyr chip that will make all your games and videos run smoothly
- an award-winning camera with optical stabilization
- a gorgeous high-definition screen that looks bright even outside in the sun
- high security protection that works in real time to protect your phone

This is a smartphone that puts the latest innovations right in your hand.

When you purchase a PrimeWave 8 this month, you can trade in your old smartphone to receive a discount of either $50 or $100 on the retail price. Check the details on our Web site.

This offer is available when purchasing a PrimeWave 8 either from our Web site or at your local participating smartphone vendor.

https://www.prime-wave.com/special-offer

Home | PrimeWave 8 | FAQ

**Offer Details**

To receive the maximum discount, your trade-in smartphone must have been manufactured within the last two years and currently be in working order. Smartphones manufactured more than four years ago are not eligible for this offer. Proof of purchase indicating the original purchase date must be submitted together with the trade-in smartphone.

**23.** According to the advertisement, what is a feature of the PrimeWave 8?
(A) Pre-installed games and videos
(B) A camera with several different lenses
(C) A highly visible screen
(D) A protective case Ⓐ Ⓑ Ⓒ Ⓓ

**24.** In the advertisement, the word "innovations" in paragraph 3, line 1, is closest in meaning to
(A) convenient products
(B) new things
(C) easy-to-use technologies
(D) luxurious items Ⓐ Ⓑ Ⓒ Ⓓ

**25.** How long is the offer available for?
(A) About one week
(B) About two weeks
(C) About three weeks
(D) About four weeks Ⓐ Ⓑ Ⓒ Ⓓ

**26.** What discount can an owner of a three-year-old smartphone likely receive?
(A) No discount
(B) $50
(C) $100
(D) $150 Ⓐ Ⓑ Ⓒ Ⓓ

**27.** According to the Web site, what document is likely required to receive a discount?
(A) A coupon
(B) A flyer
(C) An identification card
(D) A receipt Ⓐ Ⓑ Ⓒ Ⓓ

## Review Exercise

***Read these shorter versions of the advertisement and Web page details from Part 7. Fill in appropriate words in the blank spaces from the box below.***

Order the PrimeWave 8 smartphone now!
With the PrimeWave 8, you get:

- A super-fast chip for [1]__________ gaming and video streaming
- An [2]__________-winning camera with stable shooting technology
- A stunning HD screen, visible even in [3]__________
- Real-time security protection

[4]__________ to the latest tech today! Plus, trade in your old phone and [5]__________ $50 or $100. Visit our Web site for details. Available online or at select stores.

Details
For the best [6]__________, your trade-in phone must have been manufactured within the last two years and be in working condition. Broken or older phones are not [7]__________. Provide [8]__________ of purchase with your trade-in.

| | | | |
|---|---|---|---|
| (a) upgrade | (b) proof | (c) sunlight | (d) eligible |
| (e) discount | (f) award | (g) smooth | (h) save |

MEMO

UNIT 12

# News and Events

## Vocabulary Exercise

***Match each English word with its meaning in Japanese.***

**1.** upcoming (　　)　**2.** spectator (　　)　**3.** fee (　　)　**4.** alternative (　　)
**5.** in a row (　　)　**6.** resident (　　)　**7.** via (　　)　**8.** thorough (　　)
**9.** council (　　)　**10.** attendee (　　)

a.（地方）議会　b. 参加者、出席者　c. 代わりの　d. 料金
e. 連続して、一列に　f. もうすぐ来る　g. ～経由で　h. 見物人、観衆
i. 徹底的な　j. 居住者

## LISTENING SECTION

## Dictation Exercise

***Listen to the following sentences. Fill in the blank spaces.***

1. Some workers ____________________ a sign on the elevator that says “Out of order.”
2. Getting to the airport is much faster if you use the ____________________.
3. Because there are only four students in our class, we each get a lot of ____________________ attention.
4. We should ____________________ off the shelves in the storeroom. It’s dirty in there.
5. The Volunteer Week is a valuable opportunity to ____________________ your local community.

**Study Point**　Part 1　写真描写問題

人物が写っている場合の主語は、**The man** や **She**、**Some people** などが一般的ですが、何をしている人なのかが写真から明らかなときは、以下のような具体的な名称が使われることもあります。

1. **worker**　[ 作業員 ]
2. **shopper**　[ 買い物客 ]
3. **pedestrian**　[ 歩行者 ]
4. **shopkeeper**　[ 店主 ]
5. **visitor**　[ 来訪者 ]
6. **customer**　[ 客 ]

## Part 1 Photographs

2-38, 39

***Look at the picture and listen to four statements. Choose one statement that best describes the situation in the picture.***

1.

Ⓐ Ⓑ Ⓒ Ⓓ

2.

Ⓐ Ⓑ Ⓒ Ⓓ

**Study Point** Part 2 応答問題

**Are you ～ ?** や **Is it ～ ?** などのシンプルな問いかけでは、Yes や No から始まる短い選択肢は以下のようにひっかけとして使われて**不正解**なことがあります。(もちろん正解の場合もあるので、最後までよく聞くことが大切です。)

例) Are you going to eat that hamburger?

× (A) No, I'm not full.（いいえ、私は満腹ではありません）

× (B) Mexican food.（メキシコ料理です）

○ (C) You can have it.（あなたが食べてもいいですよ）

## Part 2 Question-Response

***Listen to a question or statement and three responses. Choose the best response to the question or statement.***

3. Mark your answer on your answer sheet. Ⓐ Ⓑ Ⓒ
4. Mark your answer on your answer sheet. Ⓐ Ⓑ Ⓒ
5. Mark your answer on your answer sheet. Ⓐ Ⓑ Ⓒ
6. Mark your answer on your answer sheet. Ⓐ Ⓑ Ⓒ
7. Mark your answer on your answer sheet. Ⓐ Ⓑ Ⓒ

### Study Point Part 3 会話問題

Unit 10 の Part 4 でも似たような疑問文の説明をしましたが、以下のような疑問文にはやはり注意が必要です。

**What does the speaker say they will do in the future?**
（話し手は、今後彼らは何をすると言っていますか）
* **What** does the speaker say (that) they will do ∧ in the future?
do の後ろにあった **what** が say の後ろに、さらに文頭に移動したと考えましょう。
ちなみに Unit 10 : Part 4 の Study Point で示した以下の 2 つの例文は、what が文の**主語になっている**ため、上の文とは形が異なっています。
What does the speaker say ∧ is discounted?
What does the speaker say ∧ will be discussed at the meeting?

## Part 3 Conversation

***Listen to a conversation between two people. Read the questions on your answer sheet. Choose the best answer for each question.***

8. What will take place at the culture center tomorrow?
(A) A workshop
(B) An interview
(C) A food fair
(D) A sale Ⓐ Ⓑ Ⓒ Ⓓ

9. What does the man ask the woman for?
(A) Some assistance
(B) Special equipment
(C) Copies of flyers
(D) Sewing instruction Ⓐ Ⓑ Ⓒ Ⓓ

10. What does the woman say she will do?
(A) Come early tomorrow
(B) Contact another person
(C) Help the man tomorrow
(D) Put up some flyers
Ⓐ Ⓑ Ⓒ Ⓓ

**Study Point** Part 4 説明文問題

このパートの1問目は、多くが**概要**に関するものです。例えば、最初の質問が **What is the advertisement about?** だった場合、「トークを最後まで聞かないと正解がわからないのではないか」と思う人もいるかもしれません。しかしそれは必ずしも正しいとは言えません。全体の3分の1くらいを聞けば、基本的には正解を選ぶことが可能です。**まずは最初の部分を聞いて「これかな?」と当たりを付けて、その後の断片的な情報からその答えを確定していく**、という作業が理想的かもしれません。1問目にばかり気を取られて、その後の設問の解答に影響が出ないようにしましょう。

* Unit 3: Part 4 の Study Point を改めて参照してください。

## Part 4 Talk

***Listen to a talk given by a single speaker. Read the questions on your answer sheet. Choose the best answer for each question.***

**11.** What is the broadcast about?
(A) A city award ceremony
(B) A city council election
(C) A new library
(D) A town event
Ⓐ Ⓑ Ⓒ Ⓓ

**12.** What does the speaker imply when he says, "Volunteers come in all ages and experience"?
(A) The volunteers need experience to be a volunteer.
(B) The city official should check the age requirements first.
(C) The city welcomes anyone to help.
(D) The volunteers were mostly younger.
Ⓐ Ⓑ Ⓒ Ⓓ

**13.** Where can a resident get more information?
(A) At the city hall
(B) At a city park
(C) At a library
(D) At a TV station
Ⓐ Ⓑ Ⓒ Ⓓ

# READING SECTION

## Study Point Part 5 短文穴埋め問題

### 前置詞／群前置詞

**頻出の前置詞**

① **Despite** the growing demand for local foods, it is not easy for consumers to find them.
（地元産の食品に対する需要が高まっているにもかかわらず、消費者がそれらを見つけるのは容易でない）
* **in spite of** よりも堅い言い方ですが、こちらの方が多く使用されています。

② New patients are advised to arrive ten minutes **before** their appointment time.（新患の人は予約時間の 10 分前に来るように勧められている）

③ **Before** meeting with the mayor, he practiced his presentation several times.
（市長と会う前に、彼はプレゼンテーションの練習を数回行った）
* 前置詞の before は直後に**名詞**または**動名詞**を伴います。

④ The local farmers market their crops only **through** their dedicated Web site.
（地元の農家は、専用のウェブサイトのみを通じて自分たちの農作物を販売している）
*through と似たような役割を持つ前置詞に、**along**（沿って）／**across**（横切って）／**around**（周りに）などがあります。

⑤ The company anticipates profits for the first quarter to be **between** 4 and 6 percent.（その会社は第 1 四半期の利益を 4 ～ 6% と予想している）

⑥ **Among** those who attended yesterday's local event, he was the oldest.
（昨日の地元のイベントに参加した人たちの中で、彼が最高齢だった）
***between** は「2 つのものの間」で、**among** は「3 つ以上のものの中」が原則です。

⑦ When a child is in the water, the parent or guardian must remain **within** reach of the child.
（子供が水に入っているときは、親や保護者はその子の手の届く範囲にいなければならない）
* この他に **within the budget**「予算の範囲内で」なども頻出のフレーズです。

⑧ The company provides services ranging **from** consulting **to** software development.
（その会社は、コンサルティングからソフトウェア開発にまで及ぶサービスを提供している）
*from と to はよくセットになるので、from を見つけたら to を予測しましょう。

**頻出の * 群前置詞** *2 語以上からなって 1 つの前置詞の役割を果たすもの

**due to** ～のために / **because of** ～のために / **owing to** ～のために、～のおかげで / **aside from** ～は別として / **according to** ～によれば / **along with** ～と一緒に / **apart from** ～を除けば、～を別として / **as for** ～に関しては / **as long as** ～する限り / **except for** ～を除いて / **in accordance with** ～に従って / **in conjunction with** ～と併せて / **in terms of** ～の点で / **in the vicinity of** ～の近くに

＊ Unit 9: Part 6 の Study Point も改めて参照して下さい。

## Part 5 Incomplete Sentences

***A word or phrase is missing in each of the sentences below. Choose the best word or phrase to complete the sentence.***

**14.** A community clean-up event is scheduled to be held -------- the banks of the Chuple River next weekend.
(A) through
(B) along
(C) in
(D) among　　Ⓐ Ⓑ Ⓒ Ⓓ

**15.** After the event has finished, all booths must be removed -------- the time period scheduled for clearing up.
(A) within
(B) across
(C) after
(D) from　　Ⓐ Ⓑ Ⓒ Ⓓ

**16.** Security patrols will be carried out in the -------- of the event to ensure the safety of attendees.
(A) charge
(B) regard
(C) behalf
(D) vicinity　　Ⓐ Ⓑ Ⓒ Ⓓ

**17.** Over one thousand participants took part in last Sunday's charity run -------- the wet and windy conditions.
(A) because of
(B) according to
(C) aside
(D) despite　　Ⓐ Ⓑ Ⓒ Ⓓ

**18.** -------- the weather permits, the outdoor food festival will proceed as planned tomorrow at Eastfield Park.
(A) So that
(B) As long as
(C) After all
(D) Whereas　　Ⓐ Ⓑ Ⓒ Ⓓ

### Study Point　Part 6 長文穴埋め問題

このパートでは、空所に入る最も適当な動詞を選ぶ Part 5 のような設問もあります。もし以下のような問題が出たときは、次のように考えましょう。

例）We would like you to attend the city award ceremony, which ------- on April 5.
(A) will hold　(B) is being held　(C) will be held　(D) has been held

* この問題を解くために次の 3 点を確認しましょう。
**1. 時制は何?　2. 進行形?　3. 能動態?それとも受動態?**

正解は (C) です

## Part 6 Text Completion

***Read a short text. Some words, phrases or sentences are missing from the text. Read the questions and choose the answer to complete the text.***

**Questions 19 to 22** refer to the following notice.

> **Notice**
>
> ------- (19.) road maintenance, access to Belwood Park via the main gate will not be possible during the period May 14 through May 17. The parking area next to the main gate will ------- (20.) be closed during this period. Park users should use the south gate on Melrose Avenue to enter the park while the work ------- (21.) , although please be aware that no public parking facilities are available at the south gate, and roadside parking is prohibited on Melrose Avenue. ------- (22.) . Please visit the park Web site at www.belwoodparkinformation.org.

**19.** (A) Due to
(B) Because
(C) In order
(D) Despite
Ⓐ Ⓑ Ⓒ Ⓓ

**20.** (A) too
(B) as well
(C) also
(D) addition
Ⓐ Ⓑ Ⓒ Ⓓ

**21.** (A) is carrying out
(B) was carried out
(C) is being carried out
(D) had been carried out
Ⓐ Ⓑ Ⓒ Ⓓ

**22.** (A) The parking spaces on Melrose Avenue can be viewed online.
(B) A map showing alternative parking locations is available online.
(C) Directions to the parking area at the main entrance are on our Web site.
(D) Click on the link below to see car parking fees for the south gate.
Ⓐ Ⓑ Ⓒ Ⓓ

## Study Point Part 7 読解問題

このパートの設問の中で **NOT** が入った質問は少し厄介です。内容によっては、それぞれの選択肢が本文で言及されているかどうかを確認しなければならないので、他よりも時間がかかる可能性があります。もし残り時間が少ない場合は、後回しにしてもよいかもしれません。

例 1）What is **NOT** mentioned in the notice?
（そのお知らせの中で言及されていないのは何ですか）

例 2）What is **NOT** true about the news?
（そのニュースについて真実でないのは何ですか）

例 3）What will **NOT** be featured at the local event?
（その地元のイベントで取り上げられないのは何ですか）

## Part 7 Double Passages

***Read the text and the questions following the text. Select the best answer for each question.***

**Questions 23 to 27** refer to the following notice and e-mail.

### Batik Experience at the Harton City Arts Foundation

Experience a traditional method of dyeing fabric known as batik, which is still practiced widely in countries such as Indonesia and Malaysia! The Harton City Arts Foundation is conducting a three-hour workshop on batik this Saturday, June 19, from 1:00 P.M. to 4:00 P.M. at the Harton Arts Center. The instructor is Sarina Marawan.

What to expect:

- A talk will be given about the historical origins and cultural significance of batik in Malaysian designs and clothing.
- A step-by-step lesson will cover the basics of creating a batik piece, the technique of using wax, and how to paint your own design.
- All materials will be provided and each participant will get to take home their own batik design!

Please register by sending an e-mail to admin@hartoncityarts.com (participation subject to availability). Eating is not allowed during the workshop.

Cost:
The course fee is $70.00.
Citizens age 65 and above are eligible for an automatic 50-percent discount (proof of age is required).

| To: | James Woodson |
|---|---|
| From: | Harton City Arts Foundation |
| Date: | June 15 |
| Subject: | Batik workshop |

Thank you for contacting the Harton City Arts Foundation and for your interest in our upcoming batik workshop. Unfortunately, due to popular demand, all places in the workshop are now taken and registration is closed. However, in view of the positive response to the workshop, we have invited Ms. Sarina Marawan to repeat it the month after next, and she has graciously agreed. Details will be published on our Web site shortly.

**23.** What is the purpose of the notice?
(A) To report the results of a workshop
(B) To advertise a local art-related event
(C) To inform citizens about new rules
(D) To announce the opening of an arts center
Ⓐ Ⓑ Ⓒ Ⓓ

**24.** According to the notice, what is NOT provided in the workshop?
(A) Afternoon snacks and drinks
(B) Equipment needed to create individual designs
(C) Guidance on the batik wax methods
(D) Information on batik history
Ⓐ Ⓑ Ⓒ Ⓓ

**25.** What is required to participate in this workshop?
(A) Contacting Ms. Marawan at the start of the workshop
(B) Registering at the Harton Arts Center booth
(C) Sending an e-mail to the address provided
(D) Visiting the Harton City Arts Foundation Web site
Ⓐ Ⓑ Ⓒ Ⓓ

**26.** Who can attend the workshop at a reduced fee?
(A) A 70-year old person
(B) A resident of the city
(C) A student taking an art course
(D) A volunteer of the organization
Ⓐ Ⓑ Ⓒ Ⓓ

**27.** When will the workshop be repeated?
(A) In June
(B) In July
(C) In August
(D) In September
Ⓐ Ⓑ Ⓒ Ⓓ

## Review Exercise

***Read these shorter versions of the notice and e-mail from Part 7. Fill in appropriate words in the blank spaces from the box below.***

Learn [1]_________ batik dyeing techniques at the Harton City Arts Foundation's workshop this Saturday, June 19, from 1:00 P.M. to 4:00 P.M. The [2]_________ is artist Sarina Marawan. Please check the following [3]_________ about the workshop:

- A talk on batik's history and cultural [4]_________
- Step-by-step lessons on creating your own batik item
- All [5]_________ provided, and you can take home your own design!

Register by e-mailing admin@hartoncityarts.com. Cost: $70. Seniors (65+) get a 50% discount with proof of age. No eating during the workshop.

Thank you for your [6]_________ in our batik workshop. Due to high demand, registration is now [7]_________. We'll be hosting another workshop with Ms. Sarina Marawan soon. Please [8]_________ our Web site in the near future for more information.

| | | | |
|---|---|---|---|
| (a) traditional | (b) materials | (c) visit | (d) importance |
| (e) teacher | (f) interest | (g) information | (h) closed |

MEMO

UNIT 13

# Office

## Vocabulary Exercise

*Match each English word with its meaning in Japanese.*

**1.** out of stock (　　)　**2.** budget (　　)　**3.** chat (　　)　**4.** quality (　　)
**5.** assembly (　　)　**6.** stationery (　　)　**7.** spacious (　　)　**8.** inventory (　　)
**9.** accommodate (　　)　**10.** replace (　　)

a. 在庫（リスト）　b. 文房具　c. 予算　d. 良質な　e. 在庫切れで
f. 組み立て　g. おしゃべり　h. 取り替える　i. 広々とした
j. 受け入れる、収容する

# LISTENING SECTION

## Dictation Exercise

*Listen to the following sentences. Fill in the blank spaces.*

1. I prefer working in a ________________. I like the privacy and I can concentrate on my work.
2. Who is ________________ to lead the workshop on time management?
3. My apartment is so ________________. I should move to somewhere more spacious.
4. Can we ________________ one more desk on this floor? A new person is joining next week.
5. Let's ________________ the smoking room. Nobody uses it anymore.

**Study Point** Part 1 写真描写問題

ものでも人物でもお互いの位置関係を描写する設問は、このパートで多く出題されます。見慣れないものがあれば、この機会に知っておきましょう。

**1.** The men are standing **in a row**.（その男性たちは**一列に並んで**立っている）
**2.** The women are sitting **face to face**.（その女性たちは**向かい合って**座っている）
**3.** The paintings are arranged **side by side**.（その絵は**横並びに**配置されている）
**4.** Some people are waiting **in line**.（何人かの人たちは**並んで**待っている）
**5.** They are sitting **in a circle**.（彼らは**輪になって**座っている）

## Part 1 Photographs

2-50, 51

***Look at the picture and listen to four statements. Choose one statement that best describes the situation in the picture.***

1.

Ⓐ Ⓑ Ⓒ Ⓓ

2.

Ⓐ Ⓑ Ⓒ Ⓓ

### Study Point Part 2 応答問題

注意が必要な疑問文の1つに **Do you mind if ～ ?** があります。直訳すると「**もし～すれば、あなたは気にしますか?**」なので、「～してもよいですか?」という意味になるのですが、**Don't you ～ ?** などの否定疑問文と同じように、応答は **Yes** と **No** が逆になります。

例 1） Don't you have a tablet PC?（タブレット PC を持っていないのですか）
**Yes**, I do（**いいえ**、持ってます）　**No**, I don't.（**はい**、持ってません）

例 2） Do you mind if I change the meeting to this afternoon?
（会議を今日の午後に変更してもよいですか）
**Yes**, I do.（**いいえ**、困ります）　**No**, I don't.（**はい**、いいですよ）

## Part 2 Question-Response

*Listen to a question or statement and three responses. Choose the best response to the question or statement.*

3. Mark your answer on your answer sheet. Ⓐ Ⓑ Ⓒ
4. Mark your answer on your answer sheet. Ⓐ Ⓑ Ⓒ
5. Mark your answer on your answer sheet. Ⓐ Ⓑ Ⓒ
6. Mark your answer on your answer sheet. Ⓐ Ⓑ Ⓒ
7. Mark your answer on your answer sheet. Ⓐ Ⓑ Ⓒ

**Study Point** Part 3 会話問題

図表がある場合は、音声が流れる前にそのおおよその内容を確認しておきましょう。なお、図表に関係する設問は通常、3問中1問のみです。以下の指示文がそれに該当します。

Q9. **Look at the graphic.** Which mover will they probably choose?

この部分です

## Part 3 Conversation

*Listen to a conversation among three people. Read the questions on your answer sheet and look at the graphic. Choose the best answer for each question.*

8. What does the man say about their current office?
(A) It is far from the station.
(B) It is expensive to rent.
(C) It is out of date.
(D) It is not spacious enough.
Ⓐ Ⓑ Ⓒ Ⓓ

9. Look at the graphic. Which mover will they probably choose?
(A) Ace Movers
(B) SpeedMove
(C) OfficeMove
(D) Move-in-One
Ⓐ Ⓑ Ⓒ Ⓓ

10. What does the man offer to do?
(A) Order some boxes for the move
(B) Call the moving companies
(C) Inform people of the decision
(D) Cancel a meeting about the move
Ⓐ Ⓑ Ⓒ Ⓓ

| Mover | Proposed Moving Dates |
|---|---|
| Ace Movers | October 14 ～ 15 |
| SpeedMove | October 23 ～ October 25 |
| OfficeMove | November 1 ～ November 3 |
| Move-in-One | November 29 ～ November 30 |

## Study Point　Part 4 説明文問題

このパートに限ったことではありませんが、TOEIC L&R TEST の場合、リスニングセクションの音声やリーディングセクションの本文の中で使われる語句を**言い換えた**選択肢が、正解であることが少なくありません。もちろん、全く同じ文言が正解に使用されることもあるので思い込みは禁物ですが、解答する際はよく注意しましょう。

例）音声：It's probably best to communicate by e-mail, because **I'll be traveling for work** next week.（来週出張することになっているので、おそらくEメールで連絡を取り合うのが最善でしょう）
　　問題：Why does the speaker suggest communicating by e-mail?
　　正解：**He will be out of town.**（彼は町を離れているだろうから）

## Part 4 Talk

***Listen to a talk given by a single speaker. Read the questions on your answer sheet. Choose the best answer for each question.***

**11.** What will happen next month?
(A) The company will go out of business.
(B) The company will move its office.
(C) New staff will come.
(D) The speaker will retire.　Ⓐ Ⓑ Ⓒ Ⓓ

**12.** What does the speaker think is a good idea?
(A) Canceling the project
(B) Buying a new sofa and chairs
(C) Changing the office layout
(D) Organizing an office party　Ⓐ Ⓑ Ⓒ Ⓓ

**13.** What are the listeners asked to do?
(A) Work overtime
(B) Give their opinions
(C) Choose new furniture
(D) Repair the equipment　Ⓐ Ⓑ Ⓒ Ⓓ

# READING SECTION

## Study Point Part 5 短文穴埋め問題

### 現在完了形／過去完了形

**現在完了の基本用法**

Until the office cooling system **has been fixed**, employees are allowed to work from home.

(オフィスの冷房システムが直るまで、従業員は自宅で仕事をすることが許されている)

*「修理が終わっている状態」という**完了**を表します。**結果・継続・経験**の意味もあります。

**現在完了形とよく一緒に使用される副詞(句)**

① The number of guests at the hotel has increased **since** it began offering complimentary breakfast.

(無料の朝食を提供するようになってから、そのホテルの宿泊客の数は増えた)

② The furniture store has not **yet** decided which chairs to feature during the summer sale.

(その家具店は夏のセールでどの椅子を目玉商品にするかまだ決めていない)

*上記以外に **recently**, **already**, **before**, **ever**, **never** などの副詞も使われます。

③ People have grown increasingly interested in camping **in the last 10 years**.

(キャンプに対する人々の関心はこの10年でますます高まっている)

***over the past six months**（ここ半年で）などの副詞句も使われます。

**現在完了進行形：have(has) been -ing「(今まで)ずっと～し続けている」**

• She **has been running** her office supply store for more than 20 years.

(彼女は20年以上も事務用品店を経営している)

**過去完了形：had ＋過去分詞**

• The man who called to complain **had** received a wrong item.

(苦情を言うために電話をかけたその男性は、間違った商品を受け取っていた)

*「電話をかけた」時点よりも前に「受け取っていた」ので過去完了形（大過去）が使われています。過去完了形が使われているときは、起点となる**過去を示す語句**をまず探しましょう。

**完了形が使用できないケース**

① The New York City-based design firm **was [ × has been] established** three decades ago.（ニューヨークを拠点とするこのデザイン会社は30年前に設立された）

*明らかに過去であることを示す語（句）がある場合、現在完了形は使用できません。

② Ms. Hall **will be [ × has been] supervising** the Tokyo office in the coming months in Ms. Baker's absence.

(ベイカーさんが不在の今後数ヵ月間は、ホールさんが東京のオフィスを統括します)

*未来を表す語（句）とともに現在完了形は使えません。

③ We **bought [ × had bought]** a new copier, but it broke down the next day.

(私たちは新しいコピー機を購入したが、次の日に故障してしまった)

*出来事（購入した / 故障した）を起きた順に並べる時は、どちらも過去形を使います。

## Part 5 Incomplete Sentences

***A word or phrase is missing in each of the sentences below. Choose the best word or phrase to complete the sentence.***

**14.** The office desks do not need to be replaced, even though we -------- them for more than 20 years.
(A) use
(B) are going to use
(C) were using
(D) have been using Ⓐ Ⓑ Ⓒ Ⓓ

**15.** Mr. Prakesh has not yet -------- which office layout he prefers, although we expect a decision later this month.
(A) indicate
(B) indicating
(C) indicated
(D) indication Ⓐ Ⓑ Ⓒ Ⓓ

**16.** The air conditioner in the office -------- last spring, so it is time to carry out cleaning and maintenance.
(A) was installed
(B) was installing
(C) has been installed
(D) is installed Ⓐ Ⓑ Ⓒ Ⓓ

**17.** The boxes in the corridor that ------- the storage room's door were removed last week.
(A) has blocked
(B) had blocked
(C) are blocked
(D) were blocked Ⓐ Ⓑ Ⓒ Ⓓ

**18.** Until the budget for new office furniture --------, we should make do with the old chairs and desks.
(A) approved
(B) was approved
(C) has been approved
(D) is approving Ⓐ Ⓑ Ⓒ Ⓓ

### Study Point Part 6 長文穴埋め問題

Eメールなどで相手に丁寧に注意を促したり、覚えておいてほしいことを伝える際に、以下のような表現が好んで用いられます。それぞれ細かいニュアンスの違いはあるかもしれませんが、どれも「～ですのでご注意ください」という意味だと考えて差し支えありません。

1. Please **note** that Dr. James will be taking a vacation from August 10 to 14.
2. Please **be aware** that Dr. James will be taking a vacation from August 10 to 14.
3. Please **be reminded** that Dr. James will be taking a vacation from August 10 to 14.
4. Please **remember** that Dr. James will be taking a vacation from August 10 to 14.

## Part 6 Text Completion

***Read a short text. Some words, phrases or sentences are missing from the text. Read the questions and choose the answer to complete the text.***

**Questions 19 to 22** refer to the following memo.

**MEMO**

To all employees on the 7th floor:

Please be reminded that the air conditioners on the 7th floor are scheduled ------- (**19.**) maintenance next week. This work will include cleaning the filters and ------- (**20.**) the refrigerant. In addition, to remove any risk of fire hazard, all cables will be checked and loose or broken parts will be repaired. The work ------- (**21.**) for approximately two hours, starting from 9:00 A.M. and some noise is expected. ------- (**22.**) .

**19.** (A) to
(B) into
(C) at
(D) for
Ⓐ Ⓑ Ⓒ Ⓓ

**20.** (A) remaking
(B) reforming
(C) replacing
(D) repeating
Ⓐ Ⓑ Ⓒ Ⓓ

**21.** (A) has lasted
(B) lasting
(C) will last
(D) to last
Ⓐ Ⓑ Ⓒ Ⓓ

**22.** (A) The work is scheduled to finish by 1:00 P.M. and the air conditioners will be usable after that time.
(B) The new air conditioners will provide more efficient cooling and are also energy-saving models.
(C) If you have any meetings scheduled in the morning, please consider holding them on a different floor.
(D) If you have any other IT equipment that requires repairs, please contact the maintenance department this week.
Ⓐ Ⓑ Ⓒ Ⓓ

**Study Point** Part 7 読解問題

前にも紹介したように、このパートでは**3つの文書**を扱う問題も出されます。文書の数が多くて大変なイメージがあるかもしれませんが、全5問中、1つの文書だけを読めば解ける問題も複数ありますし、2つの文書から解ける問題も複数あります。練習問題をいくつもこなしていけば必ず慣れるので、焦らず頑張りましょう。とにかく最初は以下の指示文に注目して、どれが何の文書なのかを把握することから始めましょう。

**Questions 23 to 27** refer to the following **flyer and e-mails**.

この確認から始めましょう

## Part 7 Double Passages

***Read the text and the questions following the text. Select the best answer for each question.***

**Questions 23 to 27** refer to the following flyer and e-mails.

Office Super Store

**Ergonomic Office Chair Sale**

Do you suffer from back pain, shoulder pain and headaches?
The cause may be your office chair.
For this month only we are offering a 20% discount
on any chair in the range.

**The Hansard Chair**

Available in a range of colors and fully adjustable. Made from quality materials - the back and seat are real leather.
Normal price: $240 → Sale price $192

**The Lohngren Chair**

This unique chair from Sweden is only available in the U.S. from the Office Super Store. Hand made from real wood.
Normal price: $180 → Sale price $144

**The American Ergo-Chair**

A quality chair that will last for many years, it also gets very good ratings from our customers. Self assembly required.
Normal price: $100 → Sale price $80

**The Good Back Chair**

Doctors have recommended this chair for its excellent support that will keep your back in a good posture all day.

Normal price: $150 → Sale price $120

Visit our showroom across from Central Square Station

Store Hours:

Sun. 11:00 A.M. - 7:00 P.M., Mon. ~ Fri. 8:00 A.M.- 9:00 P.M.,

Sat. 10:00 A.M. - 8:00 P.M.

| | |
|---|---|
| To: | customerservice@officesuperstore.com |
| From: | James Drew <jdrew@dmail.com> |
| Date: | July 21 |
| Subject: | Sale purchase |

Dear Sir/Madam,

I recently visited your store during the "Ergonomic Office Chair Sale" and purchased the Lohngren chair. I had hoped that it would help with my long-term back pain.

Although I was pleased with this chair at first, after using it for one day at work I have realized it is not the chair for me. The shape of the chair just doesn't provide enough support for my back.

I still wish to purchase a new ergonomic chair, so I'd like to know if it will be possible to exchange it for a different model. If there is a price difference, I would of course be happy to pay more or accept a refund on the difference.

Best regards,
James Drew

To: James Drew <jdrew@dmail.com>
From: Winifred Cahill <cahill@officesuperstore.com>
Date: July 22
Subject: RE: Sale purchase

Dear Mr. Drew,

Thank you for your e-mail.

I am sorry to hear that the chair you purchased is not to your satisfaction.

Normally, sale items cannot be exchanged, but because you are looking for an item to help with back pain, we are happy to accommodate your request this time.

However, I have checked our inventory and the only chair left is a more expensive model.

If that is acceptable, please bring the purchased item to our store as soon as possible.

Best regards,
Winifred Cahill

**23.** According to the flyer, what is indicated about the American Ergo-Chair?
(A) It is durable.
(B) It is imported.
(C) It is recommended by doctors.
(D) It is out of stock.
Ⓐ Ⓑ Ⓒ Ⓓ

**24.** What price did Mr. Drew pay for the item he has purchased?
(A) $192
(B) $144
(C) $80
(D) $120
Ⓐ Ⓑ Ⓒ Ⓓ

**25.** According to the first e-mail, what was likely the problem with the chair?
(A) The price
(B) The design
(C) The color
(D) The delivery time
Ⓐ Ⓑ Ⓒ Ⓓ

**26.** What does Ms. Cahill mention about Mr. Drew's request?
(A) It cannot be fulfilled.
(B) More information is required.
(C) An exception will be made.
(D) A decision will take some time.
Ⓐ Ⓑ Ⓒ Ⓓ

**27.** Which model of chair is available for Mr. Drew?
(A) The Hansard Chair
(B) The Lohngren Chair
(C) The American Ergo-Chair
(D) The Good Back Chair
Ⓐ Ⓑ Ⓒ Ⓓ

## Review Exercise

***Read these shorter versions of the flyer and e-mails from Part 7. Fill in appropriate words in the blank spaces from the box below.***

### Office Super Store Sale

Suffering in the office? Upgrade your chair! Discover our ergonomic chairs for better [1]_________ and posture. Get 20% off this month!

Featured Chairs:

- Hansard Chair: Fully adjustable and real [2]_________ .
  Sale: $192 (was $240)
- Lohngren Chair: Swedish-made, stylish wood design.
  Sale: $144 (was $180)
- American Ergo-Chair: Affordable, durable and [3]_________ rated. Sale: $80 (was $100)
- Good Back Chair: Doctor-recommended for excellent support. Sale: $120 (was $150)

Please [4]_________ us, opposite Central Square Station.
Open every day: Sun: 11:00 A.M.-7:00 P.M., Mon-Fri: 8:00 A.M.-9:00 P.M., Sat: 10:00 A.M.-8:00 P.M.

Dear Sir/Madam,

I recently bought the Lohngren chair in your store's Ergonomic Office Chair Sale. Although I was pleased with it, I have found it doesn't [5]_________ enough back support. I would like to exchange it for another model. If there's a price difference, I am OK to pay more or accept a [6]_________ .

Best regards,
James Drew

Dear Mr. Drew,

Thank you for your ergonomic chair purchase. Sale items usually are not exchangeable, but we're making an exception because it is for [7]__________ reasons. Regrettably, the only available model is higher priced. Please [8]__________ the purchased item to our store promptly if that is acceptable.

Best regards,
Winifred Cahill

| | | | |
|---|---|---|---|
| (a) visit | (b) return | (c) offer | (d) leather |
| (e) highly | (f) medical | (g) comfort | (h) refund |

MEMO

UNIT 14

# Review Unit 2

## LISTENING SECTION

### Part 1 Photographs

*Look at the picture and listen to four statements. Choose one statement that best describes the situation in the picture.*

1.

Ⓐ Ⓑ Ⓒ Ⓓ

2.

Ⓐ Ⓑ Ⓒ Ⓓ

## Part 2 Question-Response

***Listen to a question or statement and three responses. Choose the best response to the question or statement.***

3. Mark your answer on your answer sheet. (A) (B) (C)
4. Mark your answer on your answer sheet. (A) (B) (C)
5. Mark your answer on your answer sheet. (A) (B) (C)
6. Mark your answer on your answer sheet. (A) (B) (C)
7. Mark your answer on your answer sheet. (A) (B) (C)
8. Mark your answer on your answer sheet. (A) (B) (C)

## Part 3 Conversation

***Listen to a conversation between two people. Read the questions on your answer sheet. Choose the best answer for each question.***

**9.** Why is the woman calling?
(A) To ask about a coworker's condition
(B) To get approval on a budget item
(C) To make a doctor's appointment
(D) To remind a coworker of a deadline
(A) (B) (C) (D)

**10.** How long will the man be absent from work?
(A) A few days
(B) A week
(C) Two weeks
(D) Three weeks
(A) (B) (C) (D)

**11.** What does the woman ask the man to do?
(A) Find a replacement worker
(B) Give some information
(C) See a different doctor
(D) Come to the office
(A) (B) (C) (D)

12. Who most likely is the man?
(A) A salesperson
(B) An IT staff member
(C) The woman's assistant
(D) The woman's customer
Ⓐ Ⓑ Ⓒ Ⓓ

13. What does the woman want to finish?
(A) Her candidate interview
(B) Her presentation preparation
(C) Her research
(D) Her team's big task
Ⓐ Ⓑ Ⓒ Ⓓ

14. What does the woman mean when she says, "Well, we're going as fast as we can"?
(A) Her team will try to finish their task by the end of the month.
(B) It is not possible to finish the task.
(C) The computer system is running as fast as possible.
(D) Computer problems have delayed the project.
Ⓐ Ⓑ Ⓒ Ⓓ

## Part 4 Talk

***Listen to a talk given by a single speaker. Read the questions on your answer sheet. Choose the best answer for each question.***

15. What is being advertised?
(A) Stationery
(B) IT equipment
(C) Furniture
(D) Clothing
Ⓐ Ⓑ Ⓒ Ⓓ

16. What does the speaker mean when he says, "But you'd better be quick"?
(A) The discount is for a limited time only.
(B) The store is closing soon.
(C) Most of the products are already sold.
(D) The deadline is today.
Ⓐ Ⓑ Ⓒ Ⓓ

17. How can listeners receive a complimentary item?
(A) By spending a certain amount
(B) By applying for a credit card
(C) By entering a lottery
(D) By buying a set of items
Ⓐ Ⓑ Ⓒ Ⓓ

**18.** What will happen next month?
(A) The company will go out of business.
(B) The company will move its office.
(C) New staff will come.
(D) The speaker will retire.
Ⓐ Ⓑ Ⓒ Ⓓ

**19.** What does the speaker think is a good idea?
(A) Canceling the project
(B) Buying a new sofa and chairs
(C) Changing the office layout
(D) Organizing an office party
Ⓐ Ⓑ Ⓒ Ⓓ

**20.** What are the listeners asked to do?
(A) Work overtime
(B) Give their opinions
(C) Choose new furniture
(D) Repair the equipment
Ⓐ Ⓑ Ⓒ Ⓓ

# READING SECTION

## Part 5 Incomplete Sentences

***A word or phrase is missing in each of the sentences below. Choose the best word or phrase to complete the sentence.***

**21.** Thanks to the company's health and fitness campaign, employees are now -------- healthier than the previous year.
(A) noticeable
(B) noticeably
(C) notice
(D) noticed
Ⓐ Ⓑ Ⓒ Ⓓ

**22.** We should offer training on the new software to -------- needs it so that its introduction can go smoothly.
(A) anyone
(B) what
(C) whoever
(D) those
Ⓐ Ⓑ Ⓒ Ⓓ

**23.** The budget for advertising was -------- increased to boost in-store sales in the first quarter.
(A) further
(B) lots
(C) rather than
(D) instead of
Ⓐ Ⓑ Ⓒ Ⓓ

**24.** The promotion campaign was considered a success, -------- products sold out in stores around the country.
(A) of
(B) with
(C) at
(D) which
Ⓐ Ⓑ Ⓒ Ⓓ

**25.** After the event has finished, all booths must be removed -------- the time period scheduled for clearing up.
(A) within
(B) across
(C) after
(D) from
Ⓐ Ⓑ Ⓒ Ⓓ

**26.** The office desks do not need to be replaced, even though we -------- them for more than 20 years.
(A) use
(B) are going to use
(C) were using
(D) have been using
Ⓐ Ⓑ Ⓒ Ⓓ

## Part 6 Text Completion

***Read a short text. Some words, phrases or sentences are missing from the text. Read the questions and choose the answer to complete the text.***

**Questions 27 to 30** refer to the following advertisement.

### Soy Meat

Many consumers doubt that soy meat products can taste like real meat.

Here at Eco-Protein, we understand that.

That's -------**27.** we are offering a free trial for any of our products.

Simply register your personal -------**28.** on our Web site, choose a soy meat product that you would like to try, and we will then -------**29.** you a free sample of your choice.

That's right! You can try it – at no cost!

-------**30.** .

**27.** (A) how
(B) why
(C) what
(D) when
Ⓐ Ⓑ Ⓒ Ⓓ

**28.** (A) effects
(B) orders
(C) details
(D) affairs
Ⓐ Ⓑ Ⓒ Ⓓ

**29.** (A) send
(B) sending
(C) sent
(D) to send
Ⓐ Ⓑ Ⓒ Ⓓ

**30.** (A) Payment options include credit card and bank transfer.
(B) You will also receive a coupon to use for future purchases.
(C) After that, we will refund your money as soon as possible.
(D) Thanks to your feedback, we can improve our products.
Ⓐ Ⓑ Ⓒ Ⓓ

**Questions 31 to 34** refer to the following notice.

# Notice

-------(31.) road maintenance, access to Belwood Park via the main gate will not be possible during the period May 14 through May 17. The parking area next to the main gate will -------(32.) be closed during this period. Park users should use the south gate on Melrose Avenue to enter the park while the work -------(33.), although please be aware that no public parking facilities are available at the south gate, and roadside parking is prohibited on Melrose Avenue. -------(34.) . Please visit the park Web site at www.belwoodparkinformation.org.

**31.** (A) Due to
(B) Because
(C) In order
(D) Despite
Ⓐ Ⓑ Ⓒ Ⓓ

**32.** (A) too
(B) as well
(C) also
(D) addition
Ⓐ Ⓑ Ⓒ Ⓓ

**33.** (A) is carrying out
(B) was carried out
(C) is being carried out
(D) had been carried out
Ⓐ Ⓑ Ⓒ Ⓓ

**34.** (A) The parking spaces on Melrose Avenue can be viewed online.
(B) A map showing alternative parking locations is available online.
(C) Directions to the parking area at the main entrance are on our Web site.
(D) Click on the link below to see car parking fees for the south gate.
Ⓐ Ⓑ Ⓒ Ⓓ

## Part 7 Double Passages

***Read the text and the questions following the text. Select the best answer for each question.***

**Questions 35 to 39** refer to the following memo and e-mail.

**MEMO**

To: All Employees
From: IT Department
Date: July 28
Subject: New Office E-mail System

Please be aware that the installation date of the new office e-mail software is imminent.

As mentioned in our announcement last month, the new software will be installed on Saturday, August 1. According to the installation schedule, it will be ready to use on the Monday after that.

Please remember that your e-mails on the old system will not be automatically transferred to the new system. If you have any important e-mails, you need to save them to your cloud drive or PC hard disk by the end of July. Please note that if your cloud drive has a lot of files, it may be near the storage limit. In that case, delete some files on the cloud drive, or else just save your e-mails to your local hard disk. If you have any questions or problems, please contact Susan Wilson in the IT Department, extension 526.

To: IT Department
From: Martin Bartosz
Date: July 29
Subject: New E-mail System

Hello. This is Martin Bartosz in Sales. Regarding the new e-mail system, I have been trying to save my important mails from the old system to my cloud drive but I get an error message every time. Please advise me on how to proceed. Also, do I need to make a new password for the new system, or can I continue to use my current password?

Regards,
Martin Bartosz

**35.** Why did the IT Department send the memo?
(A) To announce a change
(B) To remind employees
(C) To obtain feedback
(D) To ask for opinions
Ⓐ Ⓑ Ⓒ Ⓓ

**36.** In the memo, the word “imminent” in paragraph 1, line 2, is closest in meaning to
(A) forthcoming
(B) important
(C) decided
(D) adjacent
Ⓐ Ⓑ Ⓒ Ⓓ

**37.** What is indicated about the new office e-mail system?
(A) It has already been installed.
(B) It will allow users to read old e-mails.
(C) It can be accessed from August 3.
(D) It requires a PC upgrade.
Ⓐ Ⓑ Ⓒ Ⓓ

**38.** According to the information in the memo, what most likely is the cause of Mr. Bartosz's problem?
(A) He forgot his computer password.
(B) He saved files to his local hard drive.
(C) He deleted files on his cloud drive.
(D) His cloud drive is nearly full.
Ⓐ Ⓑ Ⓒ Ⓓ

**39.** In the e-mail, what does Mr. Bartosz ask about?
(A) Software upgrades
(B) File permissions
(C) Login procedures
(D) Antivirus measures
Ⓐ Ⓑ Ⓒ Ⓓ

**Questions 40 to 44** refer to the following flyer and e-mails.

Office Super Store

# Ergonomic Office Chair Sale

Do you suffer from back pain, shoulder pain and headaches?
The cause may be your office chair.
For this month only we are offering a 20% discount
on any chair in the range.

**The Hansard Chair**

Available in a range of colors and fully adjustable. Made from quality materials - the back and seat are real leather.
Normal price: $240 → Sale price $192

**The Lohngren Chair**

This unique chair from Sweden is only available in the U.S. from the Office Super Store. Hand made from real wood.
Normal price: $180 → Sale price $144

**The American Ergo-Chair**

A quality chair that will last for many years, it also gets very good ratings from our customers. Self assembly required.
Normal price: $100 → Sale price $80

**The Good Back Chair**

Doctors have recommended this chair for its excellent support that will keep your back in a good posture all day.
Normal price: $150 → Sale price $120

Visit our showroom across from Central Square Station
Store Hours:
Sun. 11:00 A.M. - 7:00 P.M., Mon. ~ Fri. 8:00 A.M.- 9:00 P.M.,
Sat. 10:00 A.M. - 8:00 P.M.

To: customerservice@officesuperstore.com
From: James Drew <jdrew@dmail.com>
Date: July 21
Subject: Sale purchase

Dear Sir/Madam,

I recently visited your store during the "Ergonomic Office Chair Sale" and purchased the Lohngren chair. I had hoped that it would help with my long-term back pain.

Although I was pleased at first with the comfort and looks of this chair, after using it for one day at work I have realised it is not the chair for me. It just doesn't provide enough support for my back.

I still wish to purchase a new ergonomic chair, so I'd like to know if it will be possible to exchange it for a different model. If there is a price difference, I would of course be happy to pay more or accept a refund on the difference.

Best regards,
James Drew

To: James Drew <jdrew@dmail.com>
From: Winifred Cahill <cahill@officesuperstore.com>
Date: July 22
Subject: RE: Sale purchase

Dear Mr. Drew,

Thank you for your e-mail.

I am sorry to hear that the chair you purchased is not to your satisfaction.

Normally, sale items cannot be exchanged, but because you are looking for an item to help with back pain, we are happy to accommodate your request this time.

However, I have checked our inventory and the only chair left is a more expensive model.

If that is acceptable, please bring the purchased item to our store as soon as possible.

Best regards,
Winifred Cahill

**40.** According to the flyer, what is indicated about the American Ergo-Chair?
(A) It is durable.
(B) It is imported.
(C) It is recommended by doctors.
(D) It is out of stock.
Ⓐ Ⓑ Ⓒ Ⓓ

**41.** What price did Mr. Drew pay for the item he has purchased?
(A) $192
(B) $144
(C) $80
(D) $120
Ⓐ Ⓑ Ⓒ Ⓓ

**42.** According to the first e-mail, what was likely the problem with the chair?
(A) The price
(B) The design
(C) The quality
(D) The delivery time
Ⓐ Ⓑ Ⓒ Ⓓ

**43.** What does Ms. Cahill mention about Mr. Drew's request?
(A) It cannot be fulfilled.
(B) More information is required.
(C) An exception will be made.
(D) A decision will take some time.
Ⓐ Ⓑ Ⓒ Ⓓ

**44.** Which model of chair is available for Mr. Drew?
(A) The Hansard Chair
(B) The Lohngren Chair
(C) The American Ergo-Chair
(D) The Good Back Chair
Ⓐ Ⓑ Ⓒ Ⓓ

# Review Unit 2

学籍番号 ______________

名前 ______________

スコア　　　　/44

## Listening Section

| Part 1 | | | | |
|---|---|---|---|---|
| No.1 | Ⓐ | Ⓑ | Ⓒ | Ⓓ |
| No.2 | Ⓐ | Ⓑ | Ⓒ | Ⓓ |

| Part 2 | | | | |
|---|---|---|---|---|
| No.3 | Ⓐ | Ⓑ | Ⓒ | |
| No.4 | Ⓐ | Ⓑ | Ⓒ | |
| No.5 | Ⓐ | Ⓑ | Ⓒ | |
| No.6 | Ⓐ | Ⓑ | Ⓒ | |
| No.7 | Ⓐ | Ⓑ | Ⓒ | |
| No.8 | Ⓐ | Ⓑ | Ⓒ | |

| Part 3 | | | | |
|---|---|---|---|---|
| No.9 | Ⓐ | Ⓑ | Ⓒ | Ⓓ |
| No.10 | Ⓐ | Ⓑ | Ⓒ | Ⓓ |
| No.11 | Ⓐ | Ⓑ | Ⓒ | Ⓓ |
| No.12 | Ⓐ | Ⓑ | Ⓒ | Ⓓ |
| No.13 | Ⓐ | Ⓑ | Ⓒ | Ⓓ |
| No.14 | Ⓐ | Ⓑ | Ⓒ | Ⓓ |

| Part 4 | | | | |
|---|---|---|---|---|
| No.15 | Ⓐ | Ⓑ | Ⓒ | Ⓓ |
| No.16 | Ⓐ | Ⓑ | Ⓒ | Ⓓ |
| No.17 | Ⓐ | Ⓑ | Ⓒ | Ⓓ |
| No.18 | Ⓐ | Ⓑ | Ⓒ | Ⓓ |
| No.19 | Ⓐ | Ⓑ | Ⓒ | Ⓓ |
| No.20 | Ⓐ | Ⓑ | Ⓒ | Ⓓ |

## Reading Section

| Part 5 | | | | |
|---|---|---|---|---|
| No.21 | Ⓐ | Ⓑ | Ⓒ | Ⓓ |
| No.22 | Ⓐ | Ⓑ | Ⓒ | Ⓓ |
| No.23 | Ⓐ | Ⓑ | Ⓒ | Ⓓ |
| No.24 | Ⓐ | Ⓑ | Ⓒ | Ⓓ |
| No.25 | Ⓐ | Ⓑ | Ⓒ | Ⓓ |
| No.26 | Ⓐ | Ⓑ | Ⓒ | Ⓓ |

| Part 6 | | | | |
|---|---|---|---|---|
| No.27 | Ⓐ | Ⓑ | Ⓒ | Ⓓ |
| No.28 | Ⓐ | Ⓑ | Ⓒ | Ⓓ |
| No.29 | Ⓐ | Ⓑ | Ⓒ | Ⓓ |
| No.30 | Ⓐ | Ⓑ | Ⓒ | Ⓓ |
| No.31 | Ⓐ | Ⓑ | Ⓒ | Ⓓ |
| No.32 | Ⓐ | Ⓑ | Ⓒ | Ⓓ |
| No.33 | Ⓐ | Ⓑ | Ⓒ | Ⓓ |
| No.34 | Ⓐ | Ⓑ | Ⓒ | Ⓓ |

| Part 7 | | | | |
|---|---|---|---|---|
| No.35 | Ⓐ | Ⓑ | Ⓒ | Ⓓ |
| No.36 | Ⓐ | Ⓑ | Ⓒ | Ⓓ |
| No.37 | Ⓐ | Ⓑ | Ⓒ | Ⓓ |
| No.38 | Ⓐ | Ⓑ | Ⓒ | Ⓓ |
| No.39 | Ⓐ | Ⓑ | Ⓒ | Ⓓ |
| No.40 | Ⓐ | Ⓑ | Ⓒ | Ⓓ |
| No.41 | Ⓐ | Ⓑ | Ⓒ | Ⓓ |
| No.42 | Ⓐ | Ⓑ | Ⓒ | Ⓓ |
| No.43 | Ⓐ | Ⓑ | Ⓒ | Ⓓ |
| No.44 | Ⓐ | Ⓑ | Ⓒ | Ⓓ |

**TEXT PRODUCTION STAFF**

| | |
|---|---|
| edited by | 編集 |
| Eiichi Tamura | 田村 栄一 |
| Fumi Matsumoto | 松本 風見 |
| cover design by | 表紙デザイン |
| Nobuyoshi Fujino | 藤野 伸芳 |
| text design by | 本文デザイン |
| Hiroyuki Kinouchi (ALIUS) | 木野内 宏行（アリウス） |

**CD PRODUCTION STAFF**

| | |
|---|---|
| narrated by | 吹き込み者 |
| Howard Colefield (AmE) | ハワード・コールフィールド（アメリカ英語） |
| Jennifer Okano (AmE) | ジェニファー・オカノ（アメリカ英語） |
| Nadia McKechnie (BrE) | ナディア・マケックニー（イギリス英語） |
| Neil DeMaere (CanE) | ニール・ディマール（カナダ英語） |
| Stuart O (AusE) | スチュアート・オー（オーストラリア英語） |

**COMPREHENSIVE PRACTICE FOR THE TOEIC® L&R TEST**
**TOEIC® L&R TEST 600点への徹底演習**

---

**2025年1月20日　初版発行**
**2025年2月15日　第2刷発行**

**著　者　Jonathan Lynch**
**委文 光太郎**

**発 行 者　佐野 英一郎**

**発 行 所　株式会社 成 美 堂**
**〒101-0052　東京都千代田区神田小川町3-22**
**TEL 03-3291-2261　FAX 03-3293-5490**
**https://www.seibido.co.jp**

---

**印 刷　三美印刷株式会社**
**製 本　三美印刷株式会社**

---

ISBN 978-4-7919-7314-9

Printed in Japan